Watch Yourself

△

Other books by Matt Hern

Deschooling Our Lives (1996)
Field Day: Getting Society Out of School (2003)

WATCH YOURSELF

Why Safer Isn't Always Better

Matt Hern

NEW STAR BOOKS △ VANCOUVER △ 2007

NEW STAR BOOKS LTD.

107 – 3477 Commercial Street   1574 Gulf Road, No. 1517
Vancouver, BC V5N 4E8 CANADA   Point Roberts, WA 98281 USA
www.NewStarBooks.com

PHOTO CREDITS Dan Bushnell 4, 18, 24, 38, 58, 60, 89, 94, 117, 126, 139, 150, 154,
160. Richard Lawley 11, 21, 27, 54, 68, 70, 73, 76, 80, 92, 131. Matt Hern 14, 57, 143,
146. Selena Couture 34, 41, 46, 118. Matt Hinrichs 44. Diana Hart 160. John Hatto,
J & W Hatto Services Ltd., 106–107.

Cover design by Mutasis.com
Interior design and typesetting by New Star Books
Printed and bound in Canada by Friesens
First printing, July 2007

We acknowledge the financial support of the Canada Council, the Government
of Canada through the Book Publishing Industry Development Program, and the
Government of British Columbia through the Book Publishing Tax Credit and the
British Columbia Arts Council.

LIBRARY AND ARCHIVES CANADA
CATALOGUING IN PUBLICATION

Hern, Matt, 1968–
 Watch yourself : why safer isn't always better / Matt Hern.

ISBN 978-1-55420-021-4

1. Electronic surveillance — Social aspects. 2. Quality of life.
3. Community life. I. Title.
TK7882.E2H47   2006 303.45   C2006-900565-6

Those who would give up essential liberty to purchase a little temporary safety deserve neither liberty nor safety.

— BENJAMIN FRANKLIN, 1775

CONTENTS

ACKNOWLEDGEMENTS

Because I have been piecing this book together for so damned long, there are a lot of people who have listened to and suffered and argued with my ideas around safety over the years. I am sure that many of them will hear their voices in here. All of them deserve my gratitude.

There are too many people to list, but I am sure you will know I am thinking of you. First, much respect to New Star Books, Rolf, Carellin and Audrey in particular for having the kindness and patience to see this book through. It has been a bit of a struggle, but they hung in there with me and worked long and hard to make my ideas sort of comprehensible.

Big thanks to all the crew at the Institute for Social Ecology, all the staff, faculty and students over the years who have heard me mouthing off for many summers. And to everyone at Windsor House, the staff and parents and kids who put so much time into keeping a great place thriving. And certainly to everyone at the Purple Thistle, all the kids and (quasi) adults who continue to put so much heart and energy into the centre.

More than anything, it is my family and friends who I was thinking of when I was writing this: the ideas really only make any sense to me because of them. Dan, Sarah and Layla, Marcus, Amanda, Zak and Oscar, Stoo, Pennie and Hamish, Mark, Susan and Levi, Ashley, Keith and so many other lovely Eastsiders who make this such a great place. And my Island family: Gan, Barbara, Sean, Kelly, Kyra, Sam, David, Thirell, Riley, Fraser, Michele, David, Bronwen and Sean.

And of course, for all their love and patience, Selena and Sadie and Daisy.

This book has got to be for my folks though, Adele and Riley, for everything, and for, well, keeping me safe despite my best efforts.

My thanks to all of you.

Watch Yourself

△

PREFACE

"I was just thinking: what if we could hold things up that were bright red, or bright yellow, and he could choose? Instead of the Sameness."

"He might make wrong choices."

"Oh." Jonas was silent for a minute. "Oh, I see what you mean. It wouldn't matter for a newchild's toy. But later it does matter, doesn't it? We don't dare to let people make choices of their own."

"Not safe?" The Giver suggested.

"Definitely not safe," Jonas said with certainty. "What if they were allowed to choose their own mate? And choose wrong?"

"Or what if," he went on, almost laughing at the absurdity, "they chose their own jobs?"

"Frightening, isn't it?" The Giver said.

Jonas chuckled. "Very frightening. I can't even imagine it. We really have to protect people from wrong choices."

"It's safer."

"Yes," Jonas agreed. "Much safer."

LOIS LOWRY, *The Giver*

I've been working on this project for a disturbingly long time. And not just in the metaphorical sense, but in the practical writing, editing and researching sense. The idea for the book first struck me about eight years ago, and I began to assemble various pieces of research in a scattered and haphazard way. I had a sense, really, more than a clear idea of what I wanted. I thought that there might be a thread drawing a number of phenomena and tendencies together, a preoccupation with safety and security, and I suspected that a cultural impetus toward predictability was behind it.

The more I read, the more I poked around and the more I talked to people, the clearer it became what a monstrous and crazy inquiry I had undertaken. The idea of safety can be invoked in so many ways and has so many implications. As soon as I wrote something and began passing it around, I got fired-up responses, encouraging, questioning, challenging. It became apparent that I had struck a chord. Our relationships with security and safety go hand in hand with risk, and that dialectic is always political and usually contentious; it often pisses people off.

The idea of safety seeps and drips into almost everything, so right off I want to acknowledge that there is much, even most, that I am missing — so many "Well, what about ..." so many other possible lines of analysis. In some ways this book is inevitably incomplete and should open far more questions than it closes. I think that's a virtue for the most part. More than anything, I want to throw some doubt out there. I started asking and kept following and am a very long way from hitting bottom.

Thus, this is just one thread, one line of inquiry into the idea and ideals of security and safety. It is not true that we have reached the end of nature; it is not true that we live in the Sameness or that we have rendered our world predictable. But we're not far from it in far too many ways.

CHAPTER ONE

Possibility in the Face
of Probability

Safety first!

EVERYONE, EVERYWHERE, ALL THE TIME

You never want to look back on your life and say "I played it SAFE.*"*

MONSTER.CA TELEVISION AD

. . . the human wish, or the sin of wishing, that life might be, or might be made to be, predictable.

WENDELL BERRY, *Life Is a Miracle*

The chapter title is inspired by a comment of Isabelle Stengers in "A Cosmo-Politics: Risk, Hope, Change," in *Hope: New Philosophies for Change,* Mary Zournazi, ed. (New York: Routledge, 2002), p. 206.

1. William Leiss and Christina Chociolko, *Risk and Responsibility* (Montreal and Kingston: McGill-Queen's University Press, 1994), p. 6.

2. See, for example, Douglas's *Risk Acceptability According to the Social Sciences* (New York: Rus-

When I first stated piecing this book together and developing what I wanted to say, I thought I was going be writing about risk. And I am. In some ways this book is all about risk. In a lot of ways it is about something else entirely.

The simplest way to define risk is "exposure to the chance of loss,"[1] but that is only the barest of beginnings. There is an excellent, and huge, body of literature around risk theory and management, and as I started to read Mary Douglas,[2] Deborah Lupton,[3] Ulrich Beck,[4] Anthony Giddens[5] and so many others, I found that I kept asking a related but different set of questions. Much of what I encountered thoughtfully and incisively explored the underpinnings of why people make certain decisions about what risks to take and what constitutes a risk, but safety was too often assumed to be a de facto good, a given.

One of the first things I noticed was that the idea of safety is a surprisingly difficult one to grasp, and its meanings are consistently plastic.[6] In general, "safe" is taken to mean the opposite of "in danger" or "at risk," but of course that is never possible: we are always at risk of *something*, especially since the concepts of emotional and intellectual safety have come into use. Thus, the everyday usage tends to mean "protected from reasonable risk," but that is looser than I want. The nearest word in meaning is "secure," but that too is, at best, a temporary phenomenon. In popular discourse, people tend to refer to "safe" as a stable state, one in which all the dangers of circumstance have been warded off. It might be called safeness.

So I want to make a triangulated delineation here: safety means reducing the degree of risk in a knowable activity (say, bike riding), while security involves insulating oneself from largely unknown external dangers (like terrorism).[7] *Safeness* is an idealized state of being that encompasses both, a cocoon of protection.

In some ways I rely heavily on risk theory in this book, and in specific senses I try to depart from it. I wander through various constructionist perspectives; that is to say, I believe risk is relative, largely a matter of perception and culture. There are risks in the world, but what they are is almost entirely dependent and contingent, and always political. I am also generally in opposition to rationalist, calculated risk-management theory, what Deborah Lupton calls the realist perspective,[8] a stance that Mary Douglas describes:

> *Warm-blooded, passionate, inherently social beings though we think we are, humans are presented in this context as hedonic calculators calmly seeking to pursue private interests. We are said to be risk-aversive, but, alas, so inefficient in handling information that we are unintentional risk-takers; basically we are fools.*[9]

In part it is this kind of technocratic, calculating approach that dominates our relationships with risk in the West and, by definition, alters what we think of as safe and therefore as possible: "Instead of a sociological, cultural theory of human judgement, there is an unintended emphasis on perceptual pathology."[10]

In this book I advance another perspective on safety, one that takes a non-systematic view of risk and looks to culture and commonality instead.

I start with the premise that Western conceptions of safety are undergoing a startling transformation and that those changes are producing some deeply important cultural reverberations. Idealized applications of safety have been accelerating in intensity to the point where "safe" has emerged as a dominant criterion in both everyday and official decision making. The idea of safety has incrementally colonized every aspect of our thinking and changed the way we view all aspects of our lives and the natural world.

Whether they are red, orange and yellow colour-coded levels

sell Sage, 1985); *Risk and Blame: Essays in Cultural Theory* (London: Routledge, 2002); and Mary Douglas and Aaron Wildavsky, *Risk and Culture: An Essay on the Selection of Technological and Environmental Dangers* (Berkeley: University of California Press, 1982).

3. See Lupton's *Risk* (London: Routledge, 1999).

4. See Beck's *Risk Society: Towards a New Modernity* (London: Sage Publications, 1992); *Ecological Politics in an Age of Risk* (Cambridge: Polity Press, 1995); *World Risk Society* (Malden, MA: Polity Press, 1999).

5. See Giddens' *Modernity and Self-Identity* (Cambridge: Polity Press, 1991); *The Transformation of Intimacy: Sexuality, Love and Eroticism* (Cambridge: Polity Press, 1992).

6. See Uwe Poerksen, *Plastic Words:*

The Tyranny of a
Modular Language,
Jutta Mason and
David Cayley,
trans. (University
Park, PA: Penn-
sylvania State
University Press,
1995).

7. I'm sound-
ing like Donald
Rumsfeld here:
"We also know
there are known
unknowns..."
Sorry about that.

8. Lupton, Risk.

9. Douglas, cited
in Risk, p. 22.

10. Ibid.

of terrorist threat; "Contents hot" warning labels on coffee cups; weather hotlines; the omnipresent threat of liability lawsuits; random fear-mongering about crime or the need for home security systems, the sirens of absolute safeness continue to sing. At the same time, an army of safety experts and risk managers reduce the ideal of taking care of ourselves and each other to professional accountability and all-pervasive authority — the security guard at the library, the lifeguard telling you not to play ball at the beach, the security cameras on the corner, hygienically cleaned public spaces, and Safety First everywhere.

I believe this cultural shift is verifiable in personal, historical and quantifiable terms. It is a phenomenon most people are viscerally aware of: things are different now. At one time, not that long ago, kids went out and ran around all day, playing wherever they wanted, lawsuits were rare, and insurance was an oddly neurotic luxury. Now, "safe" is often the critical, evaluative mechanism in both public and private conversations. Safety discourse is equally powerful whether the conversation is between a mother and child, boss and worker, driver and passenger, or two lovers. A child is allowed to go outside and play if it is safe; a worker is compelled to accept a task as long as it is safe; a passenger is safe as long as she has her seat belt on; sex can happen if it's safe. Very often, and for plenty of well-articulated reasons, ideals of virtue, of good and bad, right and wrong, have been displaced by the deification of safeness.

Increasingly, doing the right thing means doing the safe thing.

ARE WE AFRAID OF THE WRONG THINGS?

There is no doubt I am suspicious of the ideal of safety. Moreover, I tend to view rhetoric about safety and security as a guise for ever-tightening social controls, especially around children. At the same time, I also recognize the reasonableness in safety-first thinking and am convinced that an increased awareness of safety and of risk reduction has improved our lives in innumerable ways. Safe sex has almost certainly slowed the advance of AIDS, work sites are better places to be, well-lit streets are less dangerous to walk at night, awareness of toxins in our food has improved our eating, etc. There are endless ways in which safety has made our lives better.

I think, however, that we can hold both a suspicion and respect. I want to examine the rise of safety and take a closer look at what safety discourses have meant and how they have become base-lines for our thinking and acting. Risk-reduction stances are never without implication, and I often see safeness running in the face of virtue, suggesting a comfortable, incapacitated blandness. Thus I will look at the nature of safety, how popular conceptions of safety have emerged and why safer isn't always better.

What I don't want to talk much about here is fear *per se*, because I think the tendency to reduce what is in front of us to psycho-logical/emotional phenomena undermines both the philosophical and political underpinnings of safeness. So many recent authors are eager to make quasi-psychological assessments of the culture at large and to suggest that we have turned into collective pantywaists, that we are just generally anxious and are making weird judgements about risk because we aren't thinking clearly.[11] According to Frank Furedi,

The perception of being at risk expresses a pervasive mood in society; one that influences action in general. It appears as a free-floating conscious-ness that attaches itself to (and detaches itself from) a variety of concerns and experiences ... there is a heightened state of readiness to react to what-ever danger is brought to the attention of the public. An understanding of

11. A crazy number of recent books have fix-ated on fear: *Culture of Fear: Risk Taking and the Morality of Low Ex-pectation*, by Frank Furedi (2002), *The Culture of Fear: Why Americans Are Afraid of the Wrong Things*, by Barry Glassner (2000), *The Abandoned Generation: De-mocracy beyond the Culture of Fear*, by Henry A. Giroux (2004), *Cel-lular Phones, Public Fears, and a Culture of Precaution*, by Adam Burgess (2003), *Face Your Fear: Living Coura-geously in a Culture Of Caution*, by Shmuley Boteach (2004), *You Have the Power: Choosing Courage in a Culture of Fear*, by Frances Moore Lappé and Jeffrey Perkins (2004). (What is it with this "culture of" thing?)

12. Frank Furedi, *Culture of Fear: Risk Taking and the Morality of Low Expectation* (London: Cassell, 1997), p. 20.

the workings of this free-floating anxiety requires an examination of the different dimensions of risk consciousness.[12]

There is something to what Furedi is saying, but there is something much deeper and stronger happening than simply people being cowed into timidity or submissiveness. Is it possible that we are irrationally scaring ourselves?[13] It's definitely true that our reaction to certain kinds of threats and dangers is disproportionate to our relatively tepid response to others. Consider that

cigarette smoking is now proven to be responsible for half a million premature deaths in the United States alone. This fact gets a modest amount of coverage in the news media, despite the fact that the number of smoking-related deaths is equivalent to three fully loaded 747 passenger jets crashing every day.[14]

That was written in 1984. In more contemporary numbers, cigarette smoking causes an estimated 440,000 deaths, or about one of every five deaths, each year in the United States alone.[15] Worldwide, "about three million people die from tobacco-related diseases each year. Within 30 years the number of tobacco-related deaths will rise to about 10 million per year. This will make tobacco the number one cause of premature death in the world."[16]

Put another way, tobacco currently causes more than 1,200 deaths every day in the United States alone. That's a September 11 every two and a half days. Why isn't the US military occupying Phillip Morris headquarters? Why aren't tobacco executives being housed at Guantanamo Bay? There are some pretty evident answers, but the questions are still good ones. And it is a clear example of how we vastly overreact to some dangers and under-react to others.

That doesn't get us all that far, though. Certainly people react more dramatically to surprising and/or large-scale danger, and of course the media loves the pornography of spectacularism a whole lot more than an ongoing, slow-moving danger. It is also true that people are much more amenable to risks that they have initiated themselves. "In voluntary activities people will accept risk that is 10 – 100 fold higher than what they would in activities or circumstances which are imposed on them without their consent."[17]

This kind of statistical analysis only gets at the issue superficially. The key is that security is never predictable and the choices we make about safety are always political. As Noam Chomsky puts it, "It's second nature for any system of power to try and inspire fear."[18] All too often people want to depoliticize risk, and that is why

13. A small wave of books working with this theme has hit us recently. For example, see H.A. Cole, *Are We Scaring Ourselves to Death?*; Laura Lee, *100 Most Dangerous Things in Everyday Life and What You Can Do About Them*; Melissa Heckscher, *Be Safe! Simple Strategies For Death-Free Living*; Martha Baer, *SAFE: The Race to Protect Ourselves in a Newly Dangerous World*. (That death-free living thing is for real, I didn't make it up. It's brilliant.)

14. John Urquhart and Klaus Heilmann, *Risk Watch:*

I think this conversation is so important, because today the very invocation of safety supersedes central political and cultural questions by posing as a de facto necessity, with the total prevention of risk a holy grail. The result is

> [a] vast hygienist utopia [that] plays on the alternate registers of fear and security, inducing a delirium of rationality, an absolute reign of calculative reason and a no less absolute prerogative of its agents, planners and technocrats, administrators of happiness for a life to which nothing happens.[19]

But culture cannot be reduced to risk management, and politics cannot be reduced to cost-benefit analyses. More prisons, constant surveillance and pervasive authority do not make us safer. Dominant contemporary notions that reify the perfectibility of safeness and the end of nature serve only to constrict the public, displacing non-official activity with private autonomous consumer zones, and, in the end, reduce us fundamentally.

DANGER LURKS EVERYWHERE

When I pay attention, I am always surprised at how often the idea of safety is the default baseline rationale for action in both professional and personal settings. I have young daughters and work with kids,[20] so I am constantly reminded how much things have changed for children and youth in the new millennium. This is perhaps the most widely understood and deeply felt consequence of the safety ethos. At the most rudimentary level, young children today are allowed vastly less freedom of certain kinds of movement than were their parents, grandparents or great-grandparents.

For example, I grew up in the country, and beginning in Grade One I walked the three miles or so home after school on my own.[21] I would never let my nine-year-old walk three miles home alone, never. When I visit my parents, who still live in the same area where I grew up, I barely let her walk to the end of the driveway unsupervised without peering out the window every fifteen seconds.

It may be that I am simply that much more neurotic than my folks (they would probably argue that), perhaps a product of my now-urban life and urban paranoia, but I don't think that's all of it. There has been a cultural shift from my parents' generation to mine that has become clearly obvious in the last thirty years.[22] Things are just different for young kids today: from bike helmets and Internet filters to designated sledding hills and GPS-equipped backpacks.

The Odds of Life (New York: Facts On File, 1984), p. xi.

15. Center for Disease Control, "Tobacco-Related Mortality: Fact Sheet," February 2004 (www.cdc.gov/tobacco/factsheets/Tobacco_Related_Mortality_factsheet.htm).

16. AADAC, "Just the Facts: Smoking Deaths" (www.zoot2.com/justthefacts/tobacco/smoking_deaths.asp)

17. Urquhart and Heilmann, *Risk Watch*, p. xii. They cite C. Starr, "Benefit-cost studies in socio-technical systems," in *Perspectives on Benefit-Risk Decision Making* (Washington, DC: National Academy of Engineering, 1972), and T.A. Kletz, "The Risk Equations: What Risks Should We Run?" *New Scientist*, May 12, 1977, pp. 320–22.

18. Cited in Geoffrey Gray, "Bush's Little Shop of Horrors," *Village*

Voice, March 12, 2002, p. 5.

19. R. Castel, "From Dangerousness to Risk," in *The Foucault Effect: Studies in Governmentality*, Graham Burchell, Colin Gordon and Peter Miller, eds. (Hemel Hempstead, UK: Harvester Wheatsheaf, 1991), cited in Lupton, *Risk*, p. 7.

20. I run an arts and activism centre for youth called the Purple Thistle (see purplethistle.ca).

21. It snowed year-round too. And there were ligers everywhere.

22. I was born in 1968.

Some of this is parentally and professionally mandated, and some of it revolves around the closing and micromanaging of public spaces. A potent combination of parental anxiety and public fear often dominates discussion about children.

In a staff meeting at the public democratic school where I once worked, the subject of tree climbing came up. One staff member was wondering what our policy about kids climbing the big trees out back should be, how far up we should allow them to go. It was a heated discussion, with some arguing that kids should be allowed to climb however high they wanted, and others claiming it was too dangerous and we should ban climbing altogether. There were suggestions that we designate a maximum height or that maybe climbing would be all right with a certain level of supervision. I thought the conversation was totally interesting and revealed much about how we perceive kids, but it ended in an altogether too familiar way.

A few years previously, in a private school in the area, a child had fallen out of a tree and died. Thus, it was pointed out to the staff, the school district would never allow us to let kids climb trees under our supervision. It would make the school board and us far too liable, and the parents of our students would likely freak out if they knew their kids were being allowed to scale towering trees. Our discussion ended with a thud. Climbing trees was too dangerous and too risky for the health of the school, given that if an accident did happen, the integrity of the institution itself would be brought into question. So tree climbing would not be allowed, a strange circumstance for a school that prides itself on the freedom it allows students. There is a logic to how that decision was reached, but the result would have been unthinkable even twenty years ago. Kids forbidden to climb trees?

This kind of story is a recognizable one and begins to illustrate the degree to which economic criteria for decision making have become the norm in public policy. The baseline is essentially a cost-benefit analysis, ostensibly useful in financial considerations, but dubious in social matters. In the case of tree climbing, the benefits are real, but smallish. It is a fun activity, but all our students could live without scaling that tree. On the other hand, the potential costs were overwhelming. If a child fell, a broken leg, arm, neck, paralysis or even death was certainly possible. So how to weigh those costs and benefits against one another? A brief thrill and fun climb versus death or maiming. Using these criteria it was an easy choice to make: stay on the ground, kiddo.

This is a slippery slope, as Dan Greenberg, one of the founders of the Sudbury Valley Free School in Massachusetts, wrote some years ago:

> The first time a twelve-year-old climbed to the top of the beech tree, our hearts stopped. There he was, calling to us proudly from seventy feet up, not quite visible through the foliage. And there we were on the ground below, with images of disaster fleeting through our minds . . .
>
> Then came "the rocks," that beautiful corner of campus strewn by Nature with large boulders. How pretty they looked — until the five- and six-year-olds decided to go in for rock climbing. How ominous they suddenly appeared!
>
> The tiny brook was next to force its attention upon us . . . We had no idea how many ways this innocent waterway could be threatening. . . .
>
> In fact, it didn't take us long to realize that, looked at from an appropriate perspective, just about anything in the environment can be dangerous. Trees, rocks, porches, roads, streams. Even our seemingly gorgeous lawn had gopher holes that lured the unwary to twist their ankles.[23]

Contemporary public policy is no longer, or perhaps is no longer allowed to be, governed by the kinds of local conversations that people and communities once engaged in to speak about safety. A cloud of litigiousness hangs over our culture, and everyone

23. Daniel Greenberg, *Free at Last* (Framingham, MA: Sudbury Valley Press, 1987), pp. 109–11.

WATCH YOURSELF

involved in any kind of public activity understands and feels it. To speak of tree climbing or the repair of a sidewalk or taking kids to the pool or building a community garden or erecting a stage or going sledding is always to speak with a lawyer whispering in your ear. Can you get sued for this? Who would hold who liable? What do you have to do to protect yourself? Contemporary discussions about what is decent, useful or fun always happen with, at least, a hallucinated lawyer listening in, making the cost side of the ledger a looming potential catastrophe.

△

The everyday effects of this kind of thinking have been felt in Ontario since 1998, when the Canadian Institute for Child Health deemed that the new Canadian Standards Association (CSA) standards should be applied to all public outdoor play areas, including those belonging to child care programs. Soon after, and in response, the province's Ministry of Community and Social Services issued a new Playground Directive, stating that all new or newly renovated child care playgrounds were required to meet all CSA standards.

Just for fun, check out this discussion of the issue from the Canadian Child Care Federation. (www.cccf-fcsge.ca/practice/policy/safety_en.html). Emphasis is mine.

> In Canada, CSA International published a revised playground standard in 1998 (CAN/CSA-Z614-98 Children's Playspaces and Equipment). This has become the Canadian benchmark for establishing requirements for play spaces and equipment. This standard has been substantially harmonized with the technical requirements of the American Society for Testing and Materials (ASTM) F 1487 as part of an international effort. Over the last few years, new playground standards have been developed for the European Economic Community, Australia/New Zealand and a committee in Japan is currently developing standards for public playgrounds. During the last few years there have been two International Playground Safety Conferences held at the University of Pennsylvania. . . . There is also a whole new climate within the regulatory community around playgrounds. In the hopes of ensuring public safety, most municipal and provincial government purchasers require suppliers to guarantee some form of compliance with an applicable voluntary standard. The most recent development in Ontario is a requirement of the Ministry of Community and Social Services that operators of licensed child care centres meet the CSA Standard. Some provincial governments are considering mandatory compliance for all public

play spaces. *In the U.S., there are currently at least six states where compliance with the Consumer Product Safety Commission Guidelines is mandated by legislation.*

When rules are in place, they must also be enforced. To that end a whole industry of playground inspector/auditors has sprung up. The U.S. National Playground Safety Institute has developed programs to create Certified Playground Safety Inspectors. In Canada, the Canadian Parks and Recreation Association has created instructional programs leading to the designation Canadian Certified Playground Inspector and the more advanced auditor level.

This meant that all playgrounds in the province had to create a safety log with action plans, designate a person to be responsible for inspections, and ensure that all materials, renovations and repairs were up to CSA standards. As well they had to put in place a supervision schedule and maintain certain staff-child supervision ratios at the playground, among much else.

As soon as insurance carriers got wind of the new directives, they refused to cover any playgrounds or facilities that were not fully compliant with the new standards. At the same time, the provincial

government refused to provide funding for playground upgrades, meaning that hundreds of play structures across the province were closed by municipalities, child care centres and non-profits unwilling or unable to risk the new exposure to liability. Of course the hardest hit were low-income neighbourhoods and smaller agencies without the capital to fund the upgrades.[24]

△

The emergence of safety-dominated thinking is not just a political/legal beast: it is a cultural shift. As Wendell Berry puts it, "our country is not being destroyed by bad politics, it is being destroyed by a bad way of life. Bad politics is merely another result."[25] I don't want to argue that a preoccupation with safety is destroying our way of life, but I do want to suggest that it is displacing much and radically altering our lives. It is certainly true that specific safety imperatives are being imposed on the general populace by eager teams of professionals, and that public policy formulation has been profoundly altered by the looming threat of lawsuits. These structural changes did not emerge out of a void, however; they grew and prospered in a cultural soil that supported the litigious logic. Then, in turn, the prevalence of legal constraints alters the way people consider their lives and surroundings, and we're off to the races.

I watched this process underway one summer at the house where I grew up, where my parents and grandmother still live. I visit often, and my kids love going to their place in the country where they can run around and explore the beach. For a long time my folks had a trampoline in the front yard, which was a huge attraction. The kids would spend hours leaping around. It was a fun thing, and often other neighbourhood kids would come down, invited or not, and play on it too. Eventually my grandma, who owns the place, heard from a lawyer or someone attuned to these things that if a child were to get injured on the trampoline, she could well be held liable.

After some thinking, she decided it wasn't worth the risk, and the trampoline was taken down and given away. The thing had existed happily and well-used for several years in the front yard without incident, but the threat of potential legal action was too much when combined with the reality that trampolines are in fact dangerous toys. So a small part of the culture shifts, and trampolines move into a liquid, probably-just-too-risky category with motorcycles, riding a bike without a helmet, mountain climbing, boxing and so forth.

I think this small story illustrates a process that is underway

24. See Ontario Coalition for Better Childcare, "What's Happening with Playgrounds?" January 2001 (www.childcareontario.org/library/playgroundsfs.html).
25. Wendell Berry is a Kentucky poet, novelist and essayist and an altogether prophetic kind of voice on a lot of subjects. This quote is from his book *What Are People For?* (San Francisco: North Point, 1990), p. 37.

across Western culture. It is a process driven by ostensible legalisms that feed people's worries, which then emerge as a belief that restricts risky activities and approaches, minimizing the possibilities of injury and pain, and supporting safety ahead of all else. The trampoline is a small thing, but it points somewhere.

It is nearly impossible to walk through any public place today without constant reminders of liability concerns in the form of rules, warnings, admonishments and assurances. Parking lots, ferries, buses, libraries, schools, hospitals, tennis courts, playgrounds, stores and restaurants all assure you that they have done everything to put safety first, so if anything happens, well, it must be your fault. But pay careful attention anyway. From the "Do Not . . ." signs in every park to the "Use With Care" labels on the underside of toys, the messages are impossible to miss. And this is the soil in which the much larger attacks on risk, like the War on Terror and the War on Drugs, can find easy root.

26. National Missing Children Services, "2003 Reference Report," (www.ourmissingchildren.gc.ca/omc/publications/ref_report_2003_e.pdf).

△

There are a variety of other factors. It is a cliché to say that we simply live in more dangerous times. In some ways this is true; in others, not at all. For example, it is a contemporary truism that there are far more creeps, pedophiles, child abductors and the like out there today, and that therefore we must watch our children extra carefully. But did you know that

> In 2003 there were three stereotypical stranger abductions in Canada. . . . In 2003, there were 39 missing children reports entered in the kidnapping [sic] by Canadian police agencies. Although this number may seem high, it should be noted that the police definition of kidnapping is that the abductor is someone other than the parents, and could, therefore, be a family member or friend. When each kidnapping report was individually analyzed, it was found that only two or three children each year are victims of stereotypical abductions. These children are most often females of elementary school age and are abducted by someone known to the family.[26]

Those kinds of statistics do not mesh at all with my gut-level perception of child abduction, nor do they support my own level of concern around this issue. Perhaps our obsession with safety has more to do with certain kinds of knowledge. It is surely true that the ubiquitous influence of the media, and its tendency toward sensationalism, bring spectacularist dangers into public view to a degree that has never before been the case. It may be that today there is a newly accepted "speakability" level around kidnappings, rape, etc. — incidents which past generations hid from public view — and that this combined with an exploding media alters people's level of knowledge and perceptions.

NORMAL PEOPLE

In his 1990 book *The Taming of Chance*, Canadian philosopher Ian Hacking investigated two complementary features of the nine- teenth century that together built a new kind of "objective knowl- edge." Hacking demonstrated that while conceptions of "chance" were displacing notions of determinism, a whole new obsession with the collection of statistical data on citizens combined to create new renditions of "normal people." By assembling a huge amount of data regarding individuals and their behaviour, officials were able to statistically describe "normal" and the variations that fell within statistical laws of dispersion.

Once "normal" can be objectively quantified and deviancy mapped, then laws of probability can be invoked and cited in deter- mining policy for a wide range of pursuits. Thus chance is "tamed" because events that were previously seen as capricious or prede- termined can be predicted within statistical laws. Crucially, "the greater the level of indeterminism in our conception of the world and of people, the higher the expected level of control."[27]

I think Hacking's analysis is important for a few reasons, some of which I will return to in subsequent chapters. For now, it is important to point out that human behaviour can be mapped in statistical totalities, made possible by

an avalanche of printed numbers. The nation-states classified, counted and tabulated their subjects anew. Enumerations in some form have always been with us, if only for the two chief purposes of government, namely taxation and military recruitment. Before the Napoleonic era most official counting had been kept privy to administrators. After it, a vast amount was printed and published. . . .

The printing of numbers was a surface effect. Behind it lay new tech- nologies for classifying and enumerating, and new bureaucracies with the authority and continuity to deploy the technology. . . .

The systematic collection of data about people has affected not only the ways in which we conceive of a society, but how we describe our neighbour. It has profoundly transformed what we choose to do, who we try to be, what we think of ourselves.[28]

27. Ian Hacking, *The Taming of Chance* (Cam- bridge, UK: Cam- bridge University Press, 1990), p. vii.

27. Ibid., pp. 2–3.

With this massive volume of statistical data widely available, the logic of probability became ascendant. Decisions, whether personal or public, began to be made with statistical inference looming over and behind them. All too often, what we think is the right thing, the good thing, to do is subsumed under an avalanche of probabilities and statistically referenced choices.

29. Ibid., p. 4.

> *Ethics is in part the study of what to do. Probability cannot dictate values, but it now lies at the basis of all reasonable choice made by officials. No public decision, no risk-analysis, no environmental impact, no military strategy can be conducted without decision theory couched in terms of probabilities. By covering opinion with a veneer of objectivity, we replace judgement by computation.*[29]

This underlies much of what I want to say about safety and how it has seeped into our discussion of everything, emboldened and reified by statistically quantifiable predictables. Safety is able to trump ethical and political discourses in part because it represents the apogee of probability analysis made everyday and tangible. "Reasonable" now means something much more than simply "common sense," and ethics are eclipsed by instrumental logic.

△

Much of our preoccupation with safety also has to do with a relentless urbanization that comes without the comprehensibility, diversity and vibrancy of genuine cities.[30] Not only cities, but much of the countryside as well is being urbanized by strip malls, big boxes, freeways and suburban housing development, so where cities and "the country" were once clearly defined, the presence of urban development now reaches far beyond city limits. With urbanization comes a whole new set of fears and expectations around personal and community safety, and many of the joys of living in the country, such as the ability to let kids run around outside unmonitored, the use of firearms and less-restrictive views of private property, become eroded.[31]

As comprehensible local places become fewer and farther between, the comfort and mutual aid that emerges in commonly held spaces is being displaced. It may be that the pervasiveness of the safety-first ethic is a reasonable response to the lack of community: where extended families and a network of neighbours once watched over children, that job now falls on individuals and families. It may be that people once felt comfortable taking more risks, knowing that if they were struck by an accident or illness, family, friends and the larger community would be there to look after them and their dependents. There are lots of other possibilities. The rise of safety may well be nothing more than the projection of white middle-class values onto society as a whole, or an odd offshoot of religion-induced guilt writ large, but I am contending here that it is much more than all that.

I also think that safety is worth exploring for a few other reasons. First, I am interested in the disabling effect a safety-first stance has on personal self-reliance, especially among children. Second, I want to look at the constriction of public and common space, and the excessive monitoring of private lives, that happens in the name of safeness. Finally, I think an obsession with safeness is shaping public policy and patterns of power in ways we're largely ignoring, and the effects are instinctually registered but too infrequently engaged.

By turning risk into an autonomous, omnipresent force in this way, we transform every human experience into a safety situation. A typical pamphlet by Diana Lamplugh, a leading British "safety expert," advises the reader to assess the risks in every situation. For instance it invites

30. See Murray Bookchin, *Urbanization Without Cities* (Montreal: Black Rose, 1992).

31. See, for example, James Kunstler, *The Geography of Nowhere* (New York: Touchstone, 1993); E.F. Schumacher, *Small is Beautiful* (New York: Harper and Row, 1973); Kirkpatrick Sale, *Human Scale* (New York: Coward, McCann and Geoghegan, 1980).

passengers of public transportation to keep alert:

The wise passenger never loses sight of the fact that public transport is still a public place. There is open access to stations. No one is vetted; everyone is acceptable as a passenger. Moreover, when we travel we are often unable to move easily and avoid trouble.

Here, the word "public" is equated with risky; the presence of the other. Unknown people are presumed to be a problem.[32]

32. Furedi, *Culture of Fear*, pp. 4–5.
33. I realize I'm not helping. Irony and all.
34. Michel Foucault, *Discipline and Punish* (New York: Vintage, 1979), p. 201.

The passage that Furedi cites was written in a country where IRA and now Tube bombings are a reality, and it must be easy to succumb to the temptation to see danger everywhere.

△

The phenomenon of safeness quickly brings to mind Michel Foucault's (massively overcited[33]) panopticon, a condition of being constantly observed, monitored and evaluated. In *Discipline and Punish*, working with a model first proposed by Jeremy Bentham, Foucault described the prison panoptical theory, an architectural arrangement in which prisoners were constantly in view of the guards, but, critically, could never see the guards themselves. Since the prisoners could never know when guards were in the tower, they never knew when they were being observed. Thus, they had to assume they were always being watched.

> *Hence, the major effect of the Panopticon: to induce in the inmate a state of conscious and permanent visibility that assures the automatic functioning of power. So to arrange things that the surveillance is permanent in its effects, even if it is discontinuous in its action; that the perfection of power should tend to render its actual exercise unnecessary; that this architectural apparatus should be a machine for creating and sustaining a power relation independent of the person who exercises it; in short, that the inmates should be caught up in a power situation of which they are themselves the bearer.*[34]

The actual surveillance is not functionally necessary. The subjects swiftly assume responsibility for their own constraints and internalize an assumption of constant monitoring so that they evolve into both prisoners and wardens.

Safeness moves from a political/bureaucratic imperative to a personal and cultural reality in much the same way. Driven in part by legalisms, authorities of all kinds develop an increasingly inclusive series of warnings and restrictions, urging citizens to

WATCH YOURSELF

be cautious. These mandates evolve from information to public encouragement to warnings to enforcement through penalties. Take the case of seat belts, for example. Driving without a belt was once the norm. Then it became questionable; now it is an infraction for which you can be pulled over and fined.

After a time, the warnings and enforcements become so ubiquitous that people assume they are always there and act accordingly. It leads to absurd circumstances. When I am camping in the bush, for example, I often find myself wondering whether I might be allowed to climb a rock or swim in a river, and my first impulse all too frequently is to look around for a sign of some kind.

△

Safeness is a cushion from the dangerous unpredictability of life and is associated with the ideal of maintaining order. Importantly, however, much of our culture toys with a simultaneous deification and vilification of this ideal. The virtuousness and primacy of safety are constantly asserted, yet acknowledged to run in the face of personal development, exciting relationships and a fulfilling life. Unnecessary risks are derided as irresponsible, but we are often encouraged to take a risk in our personal, physical, career, relationship or financial lives. "Safety first" is a mantra, but safeness as a lifestyle is dull and bland, which sort of explains the voyeuristic popularity of spectacles like live-cop shows, reality television and *Fear Factor.*

The real issue, of course, is control. Safeness is about weeding out the insecurities and the oddities of life, making it predictable and secure. All too often, the exigencies of the safety-first ethic require authoritarianism to regulate and monitor social activities. This stance easily bleeds into private lives as well, especially with children. Disallowing tree climbing, for example, may well be the safest choice for children, but it can hardly be the right one, and it requires a lot of effort on the part of adults to supervise.

To speak of safety is to speak of control, and rarely in our culture does that mean self-control. The ideal of safety is frequently conflated with what is "for your own good" as determined by parents, teachers, doctors, planners, police and public policy makers. The ubiquity of public safeness as a goal assumes the inability of individuals to make sound decisions about their own security. Soon enough, self-reliance fades and people allow officialdom to accept that burden. The self-righteousness of safety advocates almost always presents risk reduction as a self-evident truth and public requirement, and then extrapolates a social norm that answers it.

△

Recently we had some electrical work done on our rental house: we had a new circuit box installed and the electrical hook-ups moved. To complete the job an electrical inspector had to look at the work and sign off on it. After his visit (and numerous snarky asides from him about some of the DIY wiring that was done in various parts of the basement, met by pinched no-comments from me) we had a long discussion on the front porch. It was his contention and self-described mission to get sprinklers installed in every house and apartment in the city. He wanted the city to root out illegal and/or unsafe apartments, force the owners to install comprehensive sprinklers, and at the same time inspect every dwelling for unprofessional and uncertified electrical work.

His argument was simple: sprinklers work. They save lives and therefore everyone should have them. Period. He understood that sprinklers would cost thousands of dollars per house, and he acknowledged that people would be put out of their homes after landlords raised rents to pay for his proposed upgrades. He also agreed that many people would be displaced if the city did a huge sweep of illegal suites and uncertified electrical work. He insisted that it had to be done, otherwise someone was going to die.

The suggestion that living in a not-perfectly-safe funky or cheap house might be preferable to residing in a fully certified residence was incomprehensible to him. Repugnant even. Especially with kids, he mentioned pointedly to me. And frankly not a decision that people should be allowed to make. He ended the conversation with "People have to be kept safe, whether they like it or not."

It was a funny kind of interaction, both of us speaking in polite abstractions, looking out from the porch together, sort of pretending that we didn't each consider the other one's position untenable if not unethical. He was a nice guy and I enjoyed speaking with him, but the implications of his arguments illustrated something important and underlined how difficult it is to resist the dominance of safety-first thinking. The rationale that people have to be kept safe for their own good is the truck and trade of institutions that prey on those impulses, and if people want to make choices based on other values, well, too bad.

△

I believe that an investigation into the nature and emergence of safeness might shed light on our contemporary obsession with risk and help us consider its place in our lives. I hope here to repoliticize both the perceptions and practice of safety, to reassert the value and exigency of risk and to suggest that political ideals of *commonality* be returned to the center of ethical decision making, both private and public.

CHAPTER TWO

Your Home Is Your Castle:

Lock the Door, Bar the Windows

Security is a kind of death.

ATTRIBUTED TO TENNESSEE WILLIAMS

The house does not tremble, however, when thunder rolls. It trembles neither with nor through us. In our houses set close up against the other, we are less afraid.

GASTON BACHELARD, The Poetics of Space

When most people think about being safe, they think of home. They think about getting away from it all, locking the door, a shelter from the storm. When you play tag, there is always a home base where no one can get you. You score a run in baseball when you get home safely. When you are out of danger you are home free.

Much of the cocooning power of home is set against the fear of crime. The more crime looms, the more it threatens or is perceived as a threat, the more retreat into the home becomes attractive. The larger world becomes an everyone-for-themselves, dog-eat-dog milieu into which you venture to scramble for everything you can get, then scurry back home to squirrel away your hard-won rewards.

When the world is described as a fearful place full of threats and hostile others, the natural response is defence. We live in a time when gated communities and highly securitized buildings and panic rooms are the preferred choices of those with money, and everyday people do their best to approximate them, but these architectures are largely artifice. They reveal insecurity and do little to alleviate it.

I am more than familiar with the feeling of needing to secure the house. The last thing I typically do before I go to bed is lock the front door, check that the stove is turned off and make sure there are pieces of doweling in place so the windows can't slide open. The

quasi-obsessive route I make around the downstairs is long habitu-
alized now, as is the spin my mind takes as I head upstairs. I wonder
why I am so compulsive about locking the doors and then start
cataloguing all the possibilities. By the time I get to the top of the
stairs I am mentally prepping for a horde of Vikings and scheming
various defensive manoeuvres.

Even if we accept that the world is dangerous and crime ubiquitous, locking ourselves away only exacerbates our vulnerability.
It's like saying we'll all be safer when everyone owns a gun. But that
doesn't mean I'm going to stop bolting my front door.

△

It is not just metaphorically that the exaltation of our homes as
castles has become so ubiquitous. The idea of home is often placed
in antagonism to larger renditions of community and the natural
world. The ideal of the home base congeals well with conservative
values of hearth and home, solidifying the notion of individual
consumer units walling themselves off from the roiling public.
By fixating on autonomous home units that can be secured from
crime, natural forces and poverty, the weight of responsibility for
safeness shifts to families and individuals. If you don't install home
security systems, gated driveways and panic rooms, you are irre-
sponsibly exposing your children to danger.

This vision of a safely controlled existence has been considerably extended by the car and the television, both technologies that
mirror the individual isolation of the home as castle and allow
for a mediated interaction with the public, one in which all the
prurient and exotic pleasures of the world can be viewed from a
safe distance. It is easy today to move from home to car to work to
television without ever actually interacting with larger unpredictabilities. Home, car and TV bolster the lifestyle and political vision
that makes security and insularity primary virtues.

VISIBILITY AND DEFENSIBILITY

Defensible space theory makes a certain amount of sense to me,
not as an "answer" but as a way to reconsider risk. It focuses on
designing communities, buildings and public spaces for maximum
public visibility while identifying the design characteristics that
support crime. Anonymity encourages crime, but when areas of
felt responsibility are extended into public spaces, it transforms

them into common spaces. The difference is that local citizens feel they are responsible for common space, while they will leave public space to the control of officials.

That is the key, because withdrawal, whether physical (as in middle-class flight to the suburbs or hyper-securitized buildings) or psychological/intellectual (as in demanding official answers to social problems), is inevitably followed by high-intensity policing and

> the relegation of the problem of security, the traditional responsibility of the citizenry, to formally designated authority. It is no doubt impossible to imagine a modern city without a functioning police force, although their advent is as little distant as the introduction of the "Bobbys" of London in 1840. . . . But police alone can in no major way create or foster security. Society, in the persons of citizens, must adopt this function.[1]

This line of theory is typically articulated architecturally. In the 1960s, as feminist thinking was finding its way into everyday life, some campuses began to reconfigure women's dorm bathrooms with an eye to protecting against intruders and sexual assault. Designers believed this could best be done by creating single-unit bathroom and shower facilities that could be locked from the inside and were located near the ends of halls. Women could slip into the

1. Ruth Schwartz Cowan, *More Work for Mother* (New York: Basic Books, 1983), p. 14.

bathroom, lock the door behind them and shower without fear.

It soon became evident that predators were also able to sneak into the bathroom, wait for a woman to enter, and lock the door behind them, and no one would be able to hear or intervene. In response, campuses began installing bathrooms that were unlockable, collectively used and located near the middle of dorm floors, where there was the heaviest traffic. This made security a shared responsibility, and common showers collectivized the project of looking out for one another. By placing the facilities in a common area and making them permanently accessible, everyone's safety was enhanced.

It isn't hard to extrapolate from there to community. People so often speak of front porches when they talk about safe neighbourhoods because porches begin to turn the public into the common. When houses have usable and pleasant front porches or stoops, people often congregate on them in the summer, on holidays, in the evenings. When people sit on their porch and look out over the street, they tend to keep an eye on what's happening there: kids playing, couples walking, people gardening, teens hanging around. It is a picture of safety: many people keeping an eye on each other — in a parochial sense, sure, but, importantly, in a common sense.

The more we perceive our homes as security-enhanced environments to be constantly monitored for breaches, the more we insulate ourselves further, leaving ourselves vulnerable and isolated. Largely through technology, we begin to operate almost entirely as autonomously defended units.

The metaphorical home front of security can be drawn out to include the lawn, which occupies a central place in the history of post-industrial American home life and is the place where many North Americans encounter the threat of Nature most viscerally. The lawn is a battleground for legions of suburban men intent upon subduing the demons in their yards. The humble patch of grass has a mind of its own, a desire to grow thick and heavy. It is a breeding ground for weeds, five hundred square feet to fertilize, mow, pesticide, water, trim, edge, defend and hawk over.

As Paul Voykin explains in *A Perfect Lawn the Easy Way*, the emergence of a weedy lawn is a result of moral laxity and poor strategic planning in the face of constant assault.

GETTING BACK AT WEEDS

Next on our maintenance program comes weeds. These outlaws usually invade weakened lawns, which probably have become that way as a result of irresponsibility and poor maintenance by the homeowner....

CAUSES OF WEED INFESTATION

What happened? Neglect. The homeowners forgot to fertilize, or they used poor products or didn't apply enough, or they used too much and caused burning and disease. I suspect that they thought beautiful grass like this was going to take care of itself. They mowed it too short, both infrequently and with a dull mower that chewed instead of cut. Worst of all, the homeowners encouraged this ghetto of weeds by the intolerable practise of light daily sprinklings. Like their fathers before them, who sat every evening with their hoses, conversing, smoking and downing a beer or two, these homeowners have babied their lawns with hand watering or sprinklers for a brief period each evening. This destructive practise hasn't changed in thirty years.[2]

The inability or unwillingness to fight back against the weeds isn't just laziness: it's actually immoral. There are proven strategies for securing your lawn and it speaks ill of your character if you fail to follow the advice and allow your lawn to become a ghetto.

WHAT'S SAFER THAN A METAL BOX?

It wasn't until the late 1800s or even the turn of the twentieth century that the word "technology" began to replace "mechanical arts" or "practical arts" as a description of the new tools and practices that were carried in by the Industrial Revolution.[3] Leo Marx specifically ties the new term to the rise of both large, complex systems and corporate America.

During the nineteenth century, discrete artifacts or machines were replaced, as typical embodiments of the new power, by what would later come to be called "technological systems". . . . Between 1870 and 1920 such large complex systems became a dominant element in the American economy . . . They included the telegraph and telephone network; the new chemical industry, electric light and power grids; and such linked mass-production-and-use systems as the automobile industry. . . . In the era when electrical and chemical power was being introduced and these huge systems were replacing discrete artifacts, simple tools or devices as the characteristic material form of the "mechanic arts," that term was also being replaced by a new conception: "technology.[4]

With the rise of increasingly complicated systems came the development of new technocratic outlooks and philosophies, an ideal that the new phraseology reflected. "Technology" gave a sense of

2. Paul Voykin, *A Perfect Lawn the Easy Way* (Chicago: Rand McNally, 1969), pp. 40–41.

3. While the word "technology," as a systematic, inclusive term, didn't really become popularly acceptable until after the First World War, or perhaps after the Depression, there was something clearly up by the closing decades of the nineteenth century.

4. Leo Marx, "The Idea of Technology and Postmodern Pessimism," in *Technology, Pessimism and Postmodernism*, Yaron Ezrahi, Everett Mendelsohn and Howard Segal, eds. (Dordrecht: Kluwer Academic Publishers, 1994), p. 16.

common cause of cardiac arrest and will not save everyone. More lives could be saved if cardiac ...ore quickly with defibrillators. © 2005 Philips Electronics North America Corporation.

After cardiac arrest, you need help within 5 minutes. The ambulance usually takes 9.

Philips HeartStart Home Defibrillator. For the best chance of survival, a shock should be delivered within five minutes. But most sudden cardiac arrests happen at home, where help often doesn't arrive in time. So Philips designed a defibrillator for the home that can be used by people just like you. Now you can help save a life in about the time it takes to read this ad. It just makes sense. Call 1-866-333-4246 for more information on the HeartStart Home Defibrillator.

Join us on our journey at www.philips.com/simplicity

WATCH YOURSELF

PHILIP

30

smooth, humming machinery, profoundly removed from the physical toil of tools or the noisy filth of industry.

> *The lack of sensuous specificity attached to the noun, "technology," its bloodless generality, along with its habitual use in the more generalized singular form, make the word conducive to a range of reference far beyond that available to the humdrum particularities of the "mechanic" or "industrial" arts.*[5]

During the same time span, approximately 1880 to 1930, Howard Segal notes a phenomenon of technological utopian writing in the United States. In *Technological Utopianism in American Culture*, Segal documents twenty-five utopians, largely working independently and in ignorance of one another, who were producing intricate and explicit drawings and plans for new technocratic societies. Aside from the fame and influence attained by Edward Bellamy's *Looking Backward* (1888), none were very successful, but their proliferation and collective sincerity underline the nature of the times. Segal contends that "many persons today continue to equate advancing technology with utopia, and not just in America,[6] and the two contemporary tools that most radically altered the core of everyday Western culture, the television and the automobile, were both notable for their promises of virtue.

For Henry Ford and his peers, the dream of the car was articulated by the City Beautiful movement and its positivist vision of clean, ordered and safe cities. At the turn of the century, American streets were congested and dirtied by horse carriages, and cities were beset with slums and poverty, disease and overcrowding. Driven by social reformers like Charles Mulford Robinson, Herbert Ladd Towle and Daniel Burnham, urban planners and designers were overwhelmingly optimistic about flinging open cities, bathing them in light and virtue. In the automobile, the reformers saw the perfect instrument for their plans. They envisioned green, geometric suburbs, "motor colonies," with ubiquitous garages and wide, paved streets:

> *North of the business section are miles of cottages, the last word of modernity, each surrounded by lawn and shrubbery, and having — perhaps one in five — a neat garage in the rear. Shade trees line the streets; at frequent corners stand white sanitary drinking fountains, and everywhere are automobiles. Hardly one vehicle in twenty is horse-drawn. Naturally the streets of Detroit are clean. And the motor vehicles! They are radiating, imposing structures, all steel and glass. No dingy loopholes for windows, no haphazard ventilation here! The mark of the efficiency expert is seen*

5. Ibid., p. 18.
6. Howard Segal, *Technological Utopianism in American Culture* (Chicago: University of Chicago Press, 1985),

even in the buildings, and we shall find it everywhere in the work itself.[7]

This vision of orderliness was in direct contrast to the filthy, poverty-stricken and crowded state of most American cities, and the car was its physical manifestation. To own a car was to be free of the city and all its excess, insecurity and confusion.[8]

The quick rise and twenty-year sales explosion of the private car did not come without significant political help. Politicians and planners poured massive amounts of public capital into financing suburban development and car-accommodating thrusts like street widening and paving. The federal government chipped in with huge initiatives to build highways (national spending on highways topped the $1 billion mark for a single year for the first time in 1925),[9] tax breaks and sympathetic lawmaking. At the same time, the competing streetcar industry received negligible public aid and was under direct and focused attack from auto companies, especially General Motors, which actively took over electric streetcar businesses and transformed their vehicles into gas-powered buses. This particularly sordid history saw the swift decline of the mass-transit trolleys in American cities and ushered in the private car's dominance.[10]

Given the short history of the private automobile, its triumph has been almost overwhelming, and its influence is felt in every corner of the globe. The machine that was supposed to deliver us from overcrowding, congested streets, endemic filth, dangerous traveling and disorderliness has hardly fulfilled the promises its cheerleaders so confidently made less than a century ago. The private car is now synonymous with dangerous streets, polluted air and land, hazardous public spaces, frustration and myriad health and safety issues — a hard irony to swallow given its initial promises.

SEE THE WORLD FROM YOUR LIVING ROOM

If the promises of the automobile were grand in scope, the salesmen of television were no less optimistic and no less ideological about its promised social and private benefits. Like the car, the television made swift and deep inroads into Western culture, especially after the Second World War. As is the case with all great technological enterprises, the history of the television is intricately bound up with the story of its marketing. In rhetoric unsurprisingly similar to that articulated by the City Beautiful reformers, David Sarnoff, the Ford of the television, waxed poetic in 1931:

7. Towle quoted in Jane Holtz Kay, *Asphalt Nation* (New York: Crown, 1997), p. 146.

8. For more on the City Beautiful movement see Christine M. Boyer, *Dreaming the Rational City* (Cambridge, MA: MIT Press, 1983) and Peter Hall, *Cities of Tomorrow* (Cambridge: Blackwell, 1988).

9. J. Kunstler, *The Geography of Nowhere* (New York: Touchstone, 1993), p. 90.

10. Ibid., pp. 90–91.

When television has fulfilled its ultimate destiny, man's sense of physical limitation will be swept away . . . With this may come a new horizon, a new philosophy, a new sense of freedom, and greatest of all, perhaps, a finer and broader understanding between all peoples of the world.[11]

There is certainly hucksterism here, but also a good dose of the social idealism on which the selling of television was based. Like the car, the TV was going to sweep away the darkness of parochialism and demolish the constraints of time and space, ushering in a new era of security, comfort and modernity. It has always been marketed as an egalitarian technology, a tool that would give the masses access to information and sights previously available only to elites, without all the demands and dangers of actual travel. As Lee Loevinger, US federal communications commissioner, put it in 1966:

Television is not for me but for many others who do like it, but who have no time for the many things that I like. It seems to me that television is: the literature of the illiterate, the culture of the lowbrow, the wealth of the poor, the privilege of the underprivileged, and the exclusive club of the excluded masses.[12]

The idea was that people could now travel the world, seeing places and events they could never possibly have afforded to see before television. Families could stay in their chairs and still become worldly and knowledgeable in ways inconceivable before. People could accumulate experiences without ever having to experience them, roaming the world in safety.

It is an idea that has, obviously, been met with enthusiasm. The average American watches over four hours of TV per day and the television is on for seven hours and forty minutes per day in the average home. More specifically, the average American child between the ages of two and seventeen watches just under twenty hours of television per week.[13]

Are these statistics about a technology that has taken over or is out of control? Do these numbers indicate that Things are riding people? Or are they expressions of a wider cultural and social milieu that values control and predictability over all else?

It's hard to imagine anything safer than cars and television. They are brilliantly insulating technologies. Instead of walking and braving the rain, or taking the bus and braving the crowds, you can drive by yourself. You can stay home, avoid the mobs and the street, and watch television. Both tools allow for private isolation while still engaging the public sphere in a limited, controlled way. You can

11. Quoted in David E. Fisher and Marshall Jon Fisher, Tube: *The Invention of Television* (Washington, DC: Counterpoint, 1996), p. 200.

12. Quoted in Martin Mayer, *About Television* (New York: Harper and Row, 1972), p. 382.

13. TV-Turnoff Network, "Facts and Figures About our TV Habit" (www.tvturnoff.org/images/facts&figs/factsheets/Facts-Figs.pdf).

go places and witness the world without ever having to be there. It is technology rendering time and space, if not impotent, at least mastered.

14. Witold Rybc-zynski, *Home: A Short History of an Idea* (New York: Viking, 1986).
15. Ibid., p. 225.

WHEN YOU HAVE A HAMMER, EVERYTHING LOOKS LIKE A NAIL

The assumption of technological beneficence is partially tied up with assumptions about comfort. As Witold Rybczynski (drawing on John Lukacs) has pointed out, domesticity is only about three hundred years old,[14] but the idea of comfort is very much older and is a concept that has constantly been adjusted upwards. It is extremely difficult to identify comfort objectively. It's the opposite of discomfort, a term that is much more obviously measured: "The range of comfort is discovered by measuring the limits at which people begin to experience discomfort.[15]

We live in a post-scarcity time when not only can comfort be revered, but even the threat of discomfort can be extinguished. From air conditioning to towel-warming racks, Western homes are filled with devices to head off the most marginal discomforts. Marketers make sure that the spectre of discomfort is ever-present and always fixable, pointing out hassles you didn't even know you

WATCH YOURSELF

34

had, and selling you the solution in the same breath, whether it's side-mirror defoggers for cars or remotes for your stereo.

Threats to your safety are a much easier sell than small hassles, though, and it's no wonder that the initial marketing of cell phones focused on their value in emergencies, just as the current marketing of home defibrillators does. Phillips HeartStart ads show an ambulance stuck in heavy traffic, with the bolded tag line "After cardiac arrest, you need help within 5 minutes. The ambulance usually takes 9." It's a hell of an ad, and if all goes well for Phillips, we will soon be stocking our homes like emergency rooms.

The most obvious argument in favour of new technologies is always that they will make life easier, more convenient . . . safer. While in many cases they do, there are also unexpected consequences, both large and small. As Ivan Illich has pointed out repeatedly, what is lost is often difficult to regain.

> *Which type of activity women prefer — standing with other women at the common water supply for hours while they chat and engage in powerful gossip, or each one being locked in her own bathroom, cleaning the floor — I leave for them to decide.[16]*

Illich is echoing an argument best made by Ruth Schwartz Cowan in her book *More Work For Mother*. Her intensely documented history demonstrates that the avalanche of technological gadgets and appliances that have been introduced into the household have done nothing to reduce the amount of work women do, but they have altered and ghettoized housework as specifically women's and have shifted the nature of the work itself.

It's easy to get into a mindset where the acquisition of any new technology is justified if it heads off discomfort or insecurity, regardless of what it displaces. We end up creating artificial needs, things we perceive we can't do without, like home defibrillators. At some point (like right about now, I'd argue) we need to reverse field, or as Jedediah Purdy writes, "Our greatest challenge is the decision not to do what is in our power to do. We will have to do so against our present convenience. . . . We will have to do so for common reasons."[17] There are some specific approaches to the adoption of new technologies that I kind of like and think are worth considering:

> *Traditional Amish communities, often misperceived as technologically ignorant or backward, have pioneered popular deliberative processes for screening technologies based on their cumulative social effects. . . . One*

16. Quoted in David Cayley, *Ivan Illich in Conversation* (Concord, ON: Anansi, 1992), p. 156.
17. Jedediah Purdy, *For Common Things: Irony, Trust and Commitment in America Today* (New York: Knopf, 1999), p. 18

method — certainly a worthy candidate for emulation — is to place the adoption of certain new technologies under one-year probation, in order to discover empirically what the social effects will be. . . . [This should] provide crucial evidence that, given the right institutional circumstances, lay citizens can make reasonable technological decisions reflecting democratic priorities that otherwise lay fallow.[18]

18. R.E. Sclove, "Making Technology Democratic," in *Resisting the Virtual Life*, James Brook and Iain Boal, eds. (San Francisco: City Lights, 1995), p. 96.
19. Cowan, *More Work for Mother*, p. 9. I discuss this issue more in Chapter Eight.

A similarly conceived Amish practise is some communities' attitude toward the telephone. Not all Amish accept the phone into their lives, but some that have are willing to have the telephone only in a shed, away from the main living dwellings. Other communities have further rigged the phones so they can only dial out and do not ring in, meaning that control and use is limited.

The point here is not to get rhapsodic about the Amish, for there are plenty of reasons to question an often paternalistic and authoritarian culture, nor to support their theologically based rationales, but to present one living example of a disciplined relationship with tools. To even consider, for example, keeping the telephone in a shed away from the house runs in the face of contemporary consumerism, advertising and cultural expectations. Most people would probably also describe it as crazy.

As Ruth Schwartz Cowan put it, tools are not passive instruments; they have a life of their own and organize our work and tasks for us. "People use tools to do work, but tools also define and constrain the ways in which it is possible and likely that people will behave.[19] If we take safety as our operating principle and adopt new technologies without discipline, the versions of safety we get may be very different from what we imagined.

In a similar way, a particular version of the idealization of home has infected the ways we think about safety, both in the particular, but also extrapolated as metaphor to the larger world. By conceiving the home as a castle to insulate us, and then expanding that ideal farther and farther out with technology like the car and the television, we not only undermine community, but also reduce safety to a small and inadequate thing.

Beyond that, when we think of security as an absolute, as something existing outside culture, our homes become instrumentalized as just another tool for ensuring our own safety, rather than an intimate expression of our best values.

One of the most basic effects for a culture besieged by postmodern technological ironies is the continual displacement of public space by something new. Richard Sennett calls it "the paradox of isolation in the midst of visibility." In reference to

WATCH YOURSELF

modern glass buildings, he writes of "a design concept in which the wall, though permeable, also isolates the activities within the building from the life of the street. In this design concept, the aesthetics of visibility and social isolation merge.[20] Where it was once easy to describe public and private spaces, a new kind of hybrid has emerged that dominates social, especially urban, space.

This weird, paradoxical middle ground is certainly felt when we are sitting in a car downtown, visible and totally isolated, or watching TV: connected and yet disconnected. Our cultural fascination with the defeat of time and space is creating and recreating itself in a variety of arenas, displacing the idea of public and common life. The exaltation of a particular idea of home, exacerbated by the incredible array of technology at our disposal, generates a kind of all-encompassing zone whereby we are constantly ensconced in our own private spheres, hoping we're safe, imagining the worst and considering more elaborate locks on the doors.

20. Richard Sennett, *The Fall of Public Man* (New York: Vintage, 1974), p. 13.

CHAPTER THREE

Kids:

Our Most Precious Resource

"But I wanted to do it for you," Mr. Murry said. "That's what every parent wants." He looked into her dark, frightened eyes. "I won't let you go, Meg. I am going."

"No."

Mrs. Whatsit's voice was sterner than Meg had ever heard it.

"You are going to allow Meg the privilege of accepting this danger. You are a wise man, Mr. Murry. You are going to let her go."

MADELEINE L'ENGLE, *A Wrinkle in Time*

I need risks. I need to take chances. Because I am the Lydinator.

LYDIA 'THE LYDINATOR' BAIRD, AGE NINE
MARCH 24, 2005, BOCCE BALL PARK, EAST VANCOUVER

I'm standing at the top of the stairs, looking down at Third Beach, which is beautiful and perfect. It has been like 4,000 degrees all day. I can feel sweat dripping down my lower back and into my pants. The kids have sprinted ahead, heading straight for the water. I am staring at the new sign that tells me "No Camping. No Alcohol. No Dogs. No Fires. No Balls. No Inflatables."

No balls? No inflatables? At the beach? What the hell does that mean?[1]

△

Along with home, safety discourses tend to focus most frantically on children. The safety-first vocabularies we use to talk about kids and home are typically similar, rooted in comparable rationales. I'm not sure whether contemporary parents are in general more protective of their children's safety than their own parents were of theirs. It is, however, clear to me that I am more careful/neurotic about my own kids than either my parents, or their parents, were of their children.

1. Because, I was told by a helpful lifeguard, "it is impossible for the lifeguards to properly inspect all inflatables, and many are not up to CSA standards, meaning that they might actually be more of a hazard than a help. Because if a child were to take the inflatable out in the water and it were not up-to-code buoyant, it would therefore be a false security and a potential danger. And we have to keep the kids safe, don't we?" As she said that last part, she

I don't want to think of myself as an uptight parent, but it is a funny feeling to have my teenage daughter, my mother and my grandmother arrayed in a phalanx, telling me that I should chill out and let her go kayaking by herself, among other instances. I don't think this kind of anxiousness is just me; I am convinced that contemporary parents and adults are being urged, warned and threatened about safeness, both publicly and privately, in ways never before considered. The cultural inertia of safeness, the pressure that is being exerted on parents and children to control their behaviour, is redefining the act of parenting.

Every time I go out in public with kids, we are besieged by signs and warnings and video monitoring and security guards, all ostensibly to ensure our well-being. The world seems a smaller place for contemporary kids of all ages, and the prevailing wisdom is that risky behaviour just isn't worth it. The contours of adult-child discussions are complicated to trace — tricky enough personally let alone socially — but it seems to me that our current cultural stance toward children and safety is radically undermining our kids' ability to govern their own lives, and the displacement of self-reliance in favour of risk management is a perilous place to go.

I am not really interested in embarking on a sociological study to gauge quantitative levels of the practice or perception of child safety, but as a parent of youngish kids and someone who has spent the last decade and a half working intensively with children of all ages, I want to explore the "safety first" ethic that has emerged as a child rearing and supervising mantra. I wonder about all the risks I am not prepared for my daughters to take; I wonder about what my parents and grandparents would have done; and I wonder why I am so often unsure about allowing my kids the privilege of accepting danger.

Cultural shifts are often test-run on children. It is customary to iconicize kids as embodying a pure and innocent state, somehow "natural" in their instincts. Importantly, Western attitudes toward children often closely mirror our views of nature. There is often a certain kind of wildness, an unpredictability, about kids that thwarts the rational discourses of risk reduction in ways that are troubling to professional child-care people.

In the same way that (even/especially metaphorical) visits to the natural world remind us of its wildness with all kinds of disquieting movements and unknown noises, young kids transgress danger-avoidance instructions with an overwhelming curiosity and desire for exploration. All too often they just won't listen to reason. This is troubling because, just as modernity is most comfortable with

kind of raised her eyebrows at me, making sure I was agreeably in compliance. I think maybe I betrayed myself somehow.

the natural world when it is contained within clear and definable boundaries, most of us parents are comfortable when children are contained within those same comprehensible limitations.

Leaving schools out of it for now, I want to talk about how fluid interpretations of safety are consistently invoked in the name of childhood. From car seats to bike helmets to street-proofing classes, kids have been recast as precious and fragile commodities in a world bent on trashing them. More importantly, they need to be protected from trashing themselves. The ideal of safety is about predictability, a desire that runs in the face of traditional faith in the exuberance of kids and the centrality of self-reliance.

A 24/7 COP WATCHING YOUR BACK

One of the first things I did when I was researching this chapter was go to the children's section of the library and check out a pile of family-oriented videos about safety, thinking that they might illuminate contemporary attitudes toward safeness as clearly as anything else. As far as I can tell, popular safety videos fall into two main stylistic categories: productions starring and narrated by celebrities, and more straightforward, informational-type presentations.[2] In the dozens I viewed there were consistent themes and, overall, a fairly cohesive body of theory and advice.

Some of the videos I saw were very liberal and California-esque. They featured tanned, sensitive therapists urging kids and parents "to just talk about it." Many spoke of sexual abuse and tended to offer solid advice about saying "no" and talking to your parents about anyone touching you inappropriately. Others focused exclusively on more banal dangers: cutting with sharp knives, what to do in a fire, not to drink poison or heat up flammable containers. The brunt of that advice tended to be "Do not take chances." As *Child Safety* put it, "Do we do tricks on bikes? Noooo. Do we double on bikes? Nooooo. Do we ride with no hands? Noooo."[3] (Which reduced me to mooing back at the TV, "Do we watch cheesy videos and get neurotic about every fun thing? Nooooo.")

A production narrated by Gary Coleman (?!!), *For Safety's Sake*, was perhaps the most direct and crass.[4] Among his opening remarks was the semi-rhetorical query: "Boy! Wouldn't it be great if we could all have our own private police officer guarding our house 24 hours a day?" Since we don't (or, in the time of the Patriot Act, most of us hope we don't) have a cop lurking around us constantly, Gary advises us, "Do not take any chances! . . . Our best safety weapon is our knowledge." The aim here, and throughout family safety literature, can be understood as an attempt to recreate that 24/7 police officer, and not just metaphorically.

Overwhelmingly, the videos that I watched paid lip service to the idea of kids taking responsibility for their own safety, but interpreted that as "Go find an adult." The constant thematic mantra of these safety materials is "Don't take risks. Tell an adult about anything suspicious. Call 911 if you think there is any emergency." Sometimes that makes plenty of sense, and I am often thankful when my kids come and check with me about something they're unsure of. The collective cultural message of these videos, though, is hardly one of self-reliance, but rather of constant caution and maintenance. The advice is to get an adult authority and, until he or she arrives, supervise yourself as an adult would.

Compare that style of thinking with these tidbits of advice from a 1948 child-care guide *Give Your Child a Chance*. They are collected from the "Management" chapter, under the heading "Set Your Child Free":

2. For the former, see, for example, *Strong Kids, Safe Kids: A Family Guide*, directed and written by Rick Hauser, narrated by Henry Winkler(!) and featuring appearances by John Ritter, the Smurfs, Scooby-Doo, the Flintstones etc. (Paramount Pictures, 1984). For the latter, see for example *Child Safety* (National Film Board of Canada, 1994).

3. "The Binkley and Doinkel Safety Show," Part Three of *Child Safety*.

4. *For Safety's Sake*, directed by Leslie Martinson (Los Angeles: Learning Corporation of America, 1986).

Sometimes we tend to make ourselves important by keeping our children dependent. All of us tend to take from children what we need to build up our own personalities, and this is often bad for children.

Let your child play without interference. If he spanks a doll, saying "Dirty old grandpa. I have to beat you," don't interrupt with a moral lesson on respect for older people. Play is a safety valve; it enables a child to get rid of his feelings, and a child's feelings often shock adults.

Parents often try to curtail a child's activities for fear he will hurt himself. This is a risk parents have to face. Constant cautioning makes a child rebellious or, in time, makes him timid.[5]

These sentiments from more than fifty years ago are no different from those many contemporary parents would voice, but they are definitely different from how many of us act. The importance of play, and the imperative to let children figure things out on their own, has been obscured and layered over by a noisy cultural demand for supervision and maintenance.

Historically speaking, contemporary Western children are treated better, perhaps, than they ever were before.[6] Severe beatings, child labour, sexual assault and psychological degradation, once commonplace and hence unremarkable for children, have become less common. The question is whether we have passed a certain threshold and are now disabling kids, obsessing over them as "precious" in the wrong senses of that word.

PLAY SAFE NOW, KIDS

Jay Teitel argues, in "The Kidnapping of Play," that adults have appropriated children's play, taking it over for themselves, while voraciously monitoring and supervising kids' games.[7]

Teitel's description of his youth resembles what I and many of my contemporaries seem to remember of our own: unfettered days and nights running around, riding our bikes beyond our parents' call, messing around in fields, always far from adult supervision. He also describes a time when adults, particularly his father, participated in sports, but did not "play": real, serious play was always left to the children. Now, Teitel writes, adults have taken play away from the kids.

Abducting play is only the first part of our crime; holding play hostage, and then returning it to its owners in adulterated form is part two. Not only do kids play less these days than they used to; they also play differ-

5. Lenore Turner, *Give Your Child a Chance* (New York: Georgian Press, 1948), pp. 90–93.

6. See, for example, Lloyd de-Mause, *The History of Childhood* (New York: Psychohistory Press, 1974) or Charles John Sommerville, *The Rise and Fall of Childhood* (New York: Vintage, 1982).

7. Jay Teitel, "The Kidnapping of Play," *Saturday Night*, April 1999, pp. 55–60.

ently. . . . More and more, supervised play is exactly what our kids are getting. . . . It's become so commonplace — the way bicycle helmets for children have become commonplace — that we don't even think about it anymore.[8]

8. Ibid., pp. 56–57.

I think he is exactly right in claiming that what adults offer children today is "play" in an adulterated form. The essence of childhood has to be about play: relentless, every day, alone and together. And play has to be about imaginative play or it becomes something else altogether.

As a boy growing up in the country, I was like countless other kids in countless other circumstances, living and breathing to play sports. Hockey, football, basketball, tennis, lacrosse, duck on the rock, whatever . . . I just wanted to play. We played in the yard, in the lane, in the basement, in the hall, in the park, in the gym; the place was mostly irrelevant because we could think up a game anywhere. Sports are necessarily constrained by the agreements of rules and conventions, but for kids (and adults), playing in the yard is imagining the playoffs, pretending which player you are and what team you are suiting up for, hearing the crowd screaming for you.

For us, playing in the yard was arguing about who got to be Lynn Swan or Mike Bossy or World B. Free or Downtown Freddie Brown; it was seeing my glove whip out to make a save and knowing I

WATCH YOURSELF

looked just like Rogie Vachon doing it. The spontaneous play most of us remember is the great pleasure of imaginative play; in an instant we could change teams, change sports, change planets, play Calvinball, whatever. Our play was overwhelmingly non-outcome-oriented. Sure we kept score and fought about who won and lost, but there was no overriding goal in mind. We weren't practising or training or skill-building (that's turning play into careerism); we were playing for no other reason than that we wanted to.[9] We weren't developing ourselves to go pro; in our heads we were already all-stars. Serious play is without goals or outcomes, and it makes real sense only to the participants, which, as Teitel nicely illustrates, is exactly what adult supervision of play swamps. Supervised play just isn't play. It's something else again.

The common and comprehensible rationale for adult domination of kids' play is safety. It is the overwhelming reason most of us intervene, supervise and structure children's play for them. Our interventions are justified by speeding cars, abductions, concussions, eyes poked out, hurt feelings, being bullied, being scared, or broken limbs. Actually, it is not really these things; it is the spectre of these things, the worst-case scenarios, the guilt, the fear. In the era of risk-reduction analyses, our cost-benefit ratios invariably tip heavily toward hallucinated potential injuries and other disasters and the light they would cast on our parenting, but how often do we consider the costs of crowding out play?

By magnifying and fixating on the perils of childhood, our sense of reality around safeness is easily clouded, and our cheap fears and neuroses become the baseline, instead of kids' need to play. The desire to satisfy our adult twitchiness spawns an ironic paradox: by insulating children from harm, we undermine their ability to deal with it when it comes. Our culture's insistence on supervising children is not only discourteous, it is disabling.

When we create scenarios designed to reduce risk, we undermine kids' ability to discern, judge and deal with risk themselves. By setting up cooperative games and the like in order to support children's "self-esteem," we deny the possibility that they are able to cope by themselves with losing or ill-treatment.

All of us have childhood memories of losing, being bummed out, getting hurt, whatever, and we all have memories of dealing with it. The vagaries of childhood, no matter how regulated, require that kids, both individually and collectively, figure out how to deal with pain, rejection, humiliation and a thousand other torments. Our over-supervision of play strips kids of that dignity and self-reliance, which can only expose them to more risk, not less. I am coming

9. One of the most lauded and popular films of the 1990s was *Hoop Dreams*, the documentary look at two young African-American kids in Chicago growing up in basketball. As many people have pointed out, the movie was loved by white liberals everywhere because it gave form and reason and purpose to black kids' preoccupation with basketball. This movie, made by two white filmmakers looking in, is exactly the kind of misrepresentation of play that is so common among adults, particularly *faux*-anthropologists, intellectuals and the like, who are desperate to find rationales for

to believe that it is in fact not risk, but exactly this kind of direct, unmediated experience that our culture is trying to extinguish.

△

I used to belong to a great bar. It's run by a local non-profit society and is ostensibly "Members Only," although it's easy enough to get it in if you're not a member, and no great trial to join. When I first started hanging out there close to fifteen years ago, there were always kids around the place — babies, a few ten-year olds running in and out. At the time it didn't really strike me as odd. It's a loose kind of place, all dingy-basement aesthetic, and there is a community hall upstairs, so families would often attend a function and then come down for a drink afterward. Kids and adults alike could relax together after a dance or concert.

Soon after I joined, this practice was retired, and kids were no longer allowed to enter the bar. The Liquor Control people had let it slide for many years because it was a social club and the building catered to a wide range of ages, but then they began enforcing the regulations.

play — rationales aside from the simple truth that kids love basketball and want to play it. The movie is mostly unable to see that, as so many of us are unable to, and insists on representing the kids' play and love of hoops as an ultimately failed career move. Adults are fixated on interpreting children's experience of play as something meaningful in terms of quantitative outcome, not as a creative and imaginative experience worthwhile in and of itself.

Now, this bar probably isn't the greatest place for kids. It's occasionally very smoky, and there are a lot of drunk people drifting around, adults consumed with adult things. But having kids in a bar is a wonderful thing in a lot of ways; it made it a fuller and more warmly public spot, like a community living room.

Keeping kids out of bars is theoretically an issue of child protection, of buffering them from exposure to vice: the alcohol consumption, profanity, promiscuity, bad livers. The law wants that stuff contained, away from children's eyes. Excluding children from drinking establishments is largely about limiting their exposure to direct experience. Their exposure to virtual violence and vice, however, is not a problem on the whole (see video games, prime-time television, action movies, etc.), but their personal witnessing of it is a huge issue.

PEDAGOGIES OF PAIN

Implicit in many conversations about kids is a somewhat odd and dubious series of assumptions about the way people, children in particular, learn. There is a widely held belief, and a questionable one, that pain is the greatest teacher of all.

Child rearing is littered with the clichés about pain and "true" education involving everything from hot stoves, spicy food, and jungle gyms to getting in a fight or, for teenagers, drinking too much or losing a job. All of us trust these clichés on some level and resort to them at least occasionally.

When my youngest daughter, Daisy, was a toddler, we spent a lot of time in a nearby park, where she often practised her balancing by walking along a little raised chunk of concrete. It runs for about twenty feet, is raised maybe a foot, with a concrete water-play area on either side, and made an excellent and challenging balance beam for her. Daisy loved walking along it, even though the consequences if/when she fell were not insignificant. There was always the possibility that she would tumble and bash her elbow, knee or head. At times she fell painlessly, sometimes tearfully. Watching her negotiate it, I was constantly in doubt. Should I hold her hand or let her do it herself? Maybe I should hover over her and grab her as soon as she teetered. But that would take away the thrill for her, and she clearly enjoyed the game more when I let her be. Was it enough just to cheer her when she made it and comfort her when she fell?

Typically I confused myself considering the options, and she had usually moved on by the time I sorted myself out. Did she learn to balance more effectively when the consequences involved some pain? Did she focus and engage more when I was not there to catch her? What if she had cracked her head and concussed herself? Would that have been too big a price to pay for learning how to balance?

Usually I instinctively let her go or caught her, depending on how I felt in the moment, but the question of whether I was actively limiting my kid's ability to grow into herself makes me think now. Daisy is nine and my older daughter is a teenager. Is the experience of pain the best lesson?

I think the pedagogical belief that painful consequences speed learning is dubious at best. If a small child reaches for a hot burner and a parent lets her go ahead, rationalizing that she will learn effectively not to play with the stove, the consequences are complicated to guess. Who knows how a kid who burns her hand will respond: with fear, resentment or neuroses, or with solemn knowledge that she's learned not to do *that* again? It's difficult to assess the socio-psychological impacts of any given event on any given child, but the equation *Pain* = *Learning* is far too simplistic.

Thinking about this, I remember an event from my youth. I was a somewhat rowdy kid, and my buddies and I used to roam town on Saturday nights, looking for cars to steal. We'd joyride them for a while, then ditch them when we got bored. One summer night about eight of us, all sincerely drunk, rolled a big borrowed Pontiac while making a sharp turn at the bottom of a very steep hill. The car rolled, ended right side up on someone's front lawn, and we all ended up in a pile in the back seat. Incredibly, no one was hurt and everyone walked away laughing, but the whole thing scared the hell out of me.

Partly as a result of that, I have always been a careful driver myself. I have had no accidents in my twenty-plus years of driving (touch wood), including some stints as a professional driver. I consider myself cautious: I never drive after even one drink; I rarely take even small chances, like speeding deliberately; and the memory of that incident and the fear that shot through me must reside somewhere in the back of my cortex. It is indisputable to me that the panic I felt that night contributed greatly to my becoming a responsible driver, and I am unsure whether I would be as good a driver had that incident never occurred.

So what of that? In this example, the pain/learning link has some validity, but I think there's more to it than that. I do not think that suffering is the real determinant in the case of my daughter balancing, the child touching the stove, or my driving lesson.

Instead, I think maybe the real key to learning and individual development is self-driven, direct experience, the ability to experience the world on your own terms, a do-it-yourself thing. Conversely, it is the over-regulation of personal experience that constrains and restricts learning. There is a genuine satisfaction in experience, whatever the result, that is muted when mitigated by authority.

There is a very particular kind of disappointment and resentment we all feel when we know our experience has been managed for us. It is the half-pleasure, half-humiliation of getting a hit in one of those softball games where there are no strikes and everyone gets to swing until they hit. Yeah, you hit the ball, but it wasn't really you that made it happen. Everyone was going to stand there until you hit it, so where's the satisfaction in that? The attempt to manufacture self-esteem ultimately degrades it. The everybody-wins approach, the rush to avoid suffering, is insulting to individual dignity, and there is a certain kind of gracelessness and embarrassment that comes when you know your experience was planned in advance by someone else. This is a constant theme for kids today (and it is hardly limited to children).

This makes sense to me in terms of my daughter's balancing or my car fun and whatever learning we might have gleaned. They were not activities prearranged, organized and evaluated by a professional teacher. They were experiences born of our personal curiosity and exuberance and foolishness that were not very safe, but we each wanted to do them for complex reasons of our own. They may not have been advisable on one level, but they were absolutely necessary on another. It is hard to tell what either of us "learned," but they were experiences worth having, and experiences that anyone familiar with risk-reduction techniques would have rejected out of hand. (As would the owner of that Pontiac. Sorry buddy, for real.)

CONTROLLING AUTHORITY

Sometimes parents obsess about their children's safety because when their kids get hurt, they perceive it reflects badly on their own parenting and caring skills. As parents, we have an instinctive aversion to seeing our children in pain, but this instinct is one that constantly fetters our kids. We do not want our kids to get hurt, but we also understand that they need to take constant risks to grow as people. There are always limits to the kind of risks we believe our kids should accept. We are not going to let them wander around in

traffic to learn about the power of cars. The challenge is for parents, and adults in general, to enter into some kind of discourse with our fears and to offer our kids courtesy and respect.

There are so many regulatory bodies and individuals wielding official authority that often we become suspicious of all their suggestions, including benign ones. I spend the bulk of my time around kids of various ages, and, interestingly, this suspicion seems endemic to all ages. (Post-)modern kids have so much contact with random authority that it is often difficult for them to discern the difference between legitimate authority and manipulative authority. It is a key differentiation, one that John Holt, among others, has pointed to:

> *In* The Lives of Children, *[George] Dennison made the important distinction between natural authority, which rests on experience, competence, wisdom, and commitment, on the respect, trust and love of one person for the other, and official, or coercive authority, which rests only on the power to bribe, to threaten, and to punish. Many people find it hard to understand this difference, or to see that coercive authority does not complement and support natural authority, but undermines and destroys it.*[10]

10. John Holt, *Instead of Education* (New York: Dutton, 1976), p. 106.

11. I think it is inevitable that anyone living or working with kids experiences small failures every day, when our personal expectations and ethical standards are unmatched by our behaviour — the times when we turn the TV on to get some peace, when we enforce our will instead of negotiating, when we ignore the obvious solutions because we are tired. These are all reasonable and forgivable failures.

The more we as adults feel compelled to control our kids' behaviour in the name of safeness, the more I think we are admitting to and participating in a certain kind of cultural failure.[11] The supervision of play, the proliferation of authority, the lack of everyday freedom for children — these all represent a failure to trust. The more we control our children, the more we emphasize how little we think of their ability to take care of themselves. In the name of caring for children we frequently undermine their ability to care for themselves, the logical consequence of "for your own good." It is both easy and difficult to understand why we are so reluctant to allow our children the privilege of accepting danger.

IT'S NOT A BUILDING
IT'S A NEIGHBOURHOOD

CHAPTER FOUR

Neighbourhood Watch:

The Flow of Community Culture

I would emphasize the strong relation between being able to take risks and belonging. . . . It is a bit paradoxical because we usually identify risk and being detached, having nothing to lose, belonging to nothing. This is a romantic view and also a dangerous one. . . . Trust is always the condition of experimentation, of taking chances. Trust must be created for things to change.

ISABELLE STENGERS, 'A COSMO-POLITICS: RISK, HOPE, CHANGE'

I have lived all of my adult life here on Commercial Drive in East Vancouver. Both my kids were born here. I work in the neighbourhood, so I walk or ride from one end to the other almost every day. Virtually all my closest friends live nearby.

The official name of the community is Grandview-Woodlands, and it's pretty big both in size and numbers. Close to 30,000 people live here. The newspapers sometimes describe it (forebodingly) as inner city, but to my mind it is perfect: diverse, walkable, friendly, kid-friendly and relaxed. It was once largely poor and working class, but now, like many similar places, it is fighting off gentrification while still retaining a funky character. It's where I'm from.

When you say you're from here, or anywhere, you are saying something specific. It is one of the innumerable signs one offers up, from skin pigment to tattoos to clothes to accent to language, but for me it's a big one and I reference it a lot, both for myself and for others. A lot of my ideas of safety emerge from my experiences here, and in a lot of ways it's the neighbourhood that keeps me and my family and friends safe.

Sure, there are a couple of drug dealers who tend to assemble on the corner outside my house, there are packs of oft-rowdy teenagers who hang out in the park, I know there is some gang activity, but I am not involved with either gangs or drugs, and their machinations

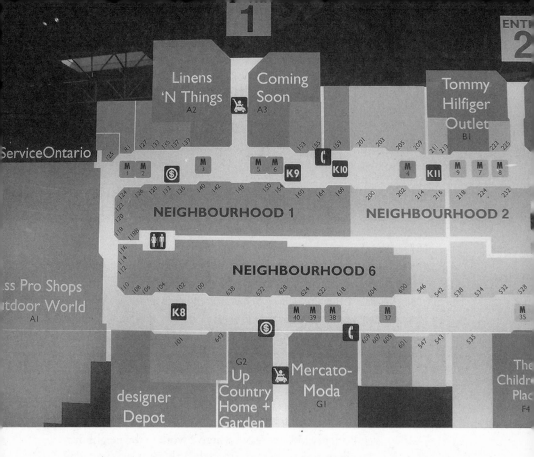

rarely affect me even tangentially. They are operating in another realm, and while it is very possible that I, or someone close to me, will be hurt or significantly impacted, it is just not something I think about. They are doing their thing, and it will continue almost exclusively parallel to my life. As Wendell Berry says:

> A community knows itself and knows its place in a way that is impossible for a public (a nation, say, or a state). A community does not come together by a covenant, by a conscientious granting of trust. It exists by proximity, by neighborhood; it knows face to face, and it trusts as it knows. . . . A community member can be trusted to be untrustworthy and so can be included. . . . But if a community withholds its trust, it withholds membership. If it cannot trust, it cannot exist.[1]

There is a section in a David Foster Wallace essay about Michael Joyce, a tennis professional, that speaks to what I am after here. Joyce is a guy who has spent his whole life totally immersed in the game, and it is really all he knows. Wallace asks him if he is happy, if he has made, and is making, a good choice.

1. Wendell Berry, *Sex, Economy, Freedom and Community* (New York: Pantheon, 1992), pp. 161–62.

The marvellous part is the way Joyce's face looks when he talks about what tennis means to him. He loves it; you can see this. . . . The love is not the love one feels for a job or a lover or any of the loci of intensity that most of us choose to say we love. . . . it's the sort of love whose measure is what it has cost, what one's given up for it. Whether there's "choice" involved is, at a certain point, of no interest . . . since it's the very surrender of choice and self that informs the love in the first place.[2]

I love the way Wallace puts this, in part because it speaks to how I think about my relationship to the neighbourhood. I could live in a lot of other places, but I don't. In this incredibly mobile world, where goods and capital and people slosh around, it feels like we can (and should) pick and choose where to live like we pick and choose a pair of shoes. Where I live just isn't a consumer choice and, in fact, is only a choice in a very limited sense.

There is a certain kind of weirdness in mythologizing the idea of community or neighbourhood. I know I am prone to this kind of romanticism. I don't want to think about the neighbourhood as a securable unit, a parochial village, but as the best of common life. Shared commitment, visibility, neighbourliness, hospitality and friendliness are much of what make a home and a community safe.

COMMUNITY AND SOCIAL ECOLOGY

In recent decades the idea of community has managed to insert itself into popular frames of reference so thoroughly that it has swiftly vaulted over cliché status and into a kind of postmodern category reserved for words that have been largely surrendered to advertising and marketers. To use the word "community" is to invoke family, neighbourliness, small-town friendliness and "honest" values in one fell swoop, a package far too attractive and useful to be left to purely vernacular usage. It is a term that is used carelessly and crassly, romantically and plaintively, but there appears to be widespread agreement that it is a thoroughly plastic term: that is to say, it can mean almost anything.[3]

It is this plasticity that hollows out the idea that once informed the word. In everyday usage, "community" describes whatever anyone feels like: loose affiliations (the Vancouver business community), structured associations of any size (the European Economic Community), largely unstructured networks of interest (the community of women scholars), local projects (the school community), housing developments (retirement communities),

2. David Foster Wallace, "Tennis Player Michael Joyce's Professional Artistry as a Paradigm of Certain Stuff about Choice, Freedom, Limitation, Joy, Grotesquerie and Human Completeness," in *A Supposedly Fun Thing I'll Never Do Again* (New York: Little, Brown, 1997), p. 228.

3. See Uwe Poerksen, *Plastic Words: The Tyranny of a Modular Language*, Jutte Mason and David Cayley, trans. (University Park, PA: Penn State University Press, 1995).

shopping districts . . . whatever. When the APEC Summit was held in Vancouver in 1997, bringing in eighteen heads of state representing countries around the Pacific Rim, one of the widely distributed promotional posters was headlined "APEC: tying the community together."

Part of what makes "community" such an appealing and marketable ideal is its generalized ambiguity. It evokes a swathe of traditional and comforting values, but rarely anything specific. Its cultural location is surprisingly liquid, but certainly the idea is affiliated with warm ideas of safety: unlocked doors, friendly people, kids playing in the street. This kind of community is frequently referenced in ads for condos ("It's not just a building, it's a community!") and restricted living situations ("The kind of adult community you deserve"), and it surfaces often in new ecological literatures (urban villages, etc.). In many ways, lasting and meaningful discourse about safety has to be about the nature of community.

Much of the popular ideal of community implies shared value systems, suggesting an enlarged version of the understandings that members of a family have with one another. Discourse about community is often conflated with "home," and community itself is often thought of as an extension of home, a place where people know you, understand your history and will forgive you for your transgressions.

These "big home" renditions of community have been challenged frequently by those who see them as binding, restrictive and likely regressive. Some feminists have made it clear that the homes in which many women grew up were hardly decent models for social organization.

> *The historical transformation that gives rise to the modernist vision of "home" as the utopian and sheltered place of safety, for which we supposedly all yearn, draws upon an exclusionary, territorializing, xenophobic, premodern and patriarchal cult of "home" that predates and prefixes it.* [4]

For those who experienced abuse, rejection, violence, insecurity, control and degradation as standard home fare, the argument that community should be like a "big home" often sounds ignorant at best.

Similarly, if small-town values are synonymous with friendliness and mutual aid, they can also imply racism, homophobia, wife beating and the violent distrust of Otherness. There are plenty of reasons to be suspicious of the value of "big home" community arguments when so many of us have had to flee the stifling confines

4. Anna Antonopoulos, "The Politics of Home," in *Who Is This 'We'?* Eleanor Godway and Geraldine Finn, eds. (Montreal: Black Rose, 1994), p. 57.

WATCH YOURSELF

of our hometowns for other places, often huge cities, where we can "feel more at home." In this context, the space that "home" once occupied in definitions of community is now frequently filled by the concept of "interest," an interpretation popular among liberals and the new academic communitarians, which makes it possible to say something like "virtual communities" or "online communities."

In many ways, the ideal of community seems outdated in the current era, which is characterized by the unimpeded flow of huge chunks of capital, the globalization of marketplaces and culture, and the increasingly oligarchic tendencies of corporate and governmental elites. Our culture tends to deify fluidity and mobility. Instead of the security of "home," family or friends, contemporary safety seems to stem from individuals' ability to slip, slide and shimmy easily away from dangerous commitments, lousy jobs, unhappy homes and unsatisfactory neighbourhoods or social groups: there is always somewhere else to go, someone else to hang out with, another job to find, a better place to shop.

This is the lived function of late-capitalist cultural practice. Personal mobility and consumerist ideology inform so many of our beliefs about the good life that a commitment to place often seems pastorally wistful or naively absurd. Still, evocations of community continue to have resilient power and resonance in both popular and official discourses, in part perhaps because political conversations are best rooted in local places.

The link between community and democracy is an inextricable one: they require one another. Local politics, local languages and local relationships have to survive and thrive for the development of understandable democracies, which can only emerge in the context of community. This is not to advocate isolationism and parochialism, but to argue that community is necessarily the basis for an ecological and decent society, and that universalizing global logics and languages necessarily undermines the conditions for community.

Importantly, to speak of contemporary community is to speak of interdependence. We have to be able to expand any invocation of community control and direct democracies beyond localism and toward a vision of interdependence. No community anywhere can live in a vacuum; the results of our collective behaviours — from downstream pollution to highways to fishing — inevitably affect our neighbours. In any attempt to describe community, we have to acknowledge that isolation is impossible.

Among a chorus of regionalists and bioregionalists, most of

whom build on the writings of Patrick Geddes and Lewis Mumford, Murray Bookchin has contributed some of the best descriptions of how community has to transcend simple localism:

> *Together with decentralization, approximations to self-sufficiency, humanly scaled communities, ecotechnologies and the like, there is a compelling need for democratic and truly communitarian forms of interdependence — in short, for libertarian forms of confederalism. . . . Confederation must be conceived as an extension of a form of participatory administration. . . . Confederalism is thus a way of perpetuating the interdependence that should exist among communities and regions — indeed, it is a way of democratizing that interdependence without surrendering the principle of local control.[5]*

To resist universalizing and globalizing agendas is not to revert to mere parochialism, but to speak to the ecological and democratic necessities of local control and interrelatedness. Any discussion of community is necessarily a discussion of limits and what it means to limit concentrations of power, to limit growth and to limit spheres of political control.

I know this discussion of community is a little abstract, but grappling with the ideal of community is essential for understanding what we do mean, and what we should mean, by safety. Many people have tried to define community, and it is worth checking out a few of those definitions here because in a lot of ways community is all about who is in and who is out. That is one piece of keeping ourselves safe: who do we allow around us, who do we interact with, who is allowed "here" and how are those boundaries enforced? The idea of community is about belonging and trust, and often those values are (kind of ironically) best defined in the negative: who is not invited here, what activities are unacceptable and who don't we trust.

WHO'S IN, WHO'S OUT

To retain its force, "community" *has* to refer to a geographical place, a place to which residents have made a long-term commitment. To say that there is "a nation-wide community of scholars" or a "sporting community" or a "virtual community" or a "business community" is absurd. Those names refer to associations or networks or affiliations, important endeavours that are not to be belittled, but they are not communities.

5. Murray Bookchin, *Urbanization Without Cities* (Montreal: Black Rose, 1992), pp. 296–98

If "community" is to mean anything at all, it has to mean a placed people, and more than that, as Wendell Berry writes:

> If we speak of a healthy community, we cannot be speaking of a community that is merely human. We are talking about a neighborhood of humans in a place, plus the place itself: its soil, its water, its air, and all the families and tribes of nonhuman creatures that belong to it. If the place is well preserved, if its entire membership, natural and human, is present in it, and if the human economy is in practical harmony with the nature of the place, then the community is healthy.[6]

In his book *The Struggle for Community*, Allan Heskin describes three versions of community co-existing not so peaceably in the Route 2 housing project of Los Angeles: the *populist*, the *pluralist* and the *clientelists*.

Heskin describes the populists as hoping for the creation of "functional communities . . . co-ops that would be an oasis. . . . They wanted to create communities not in ties of friendship, but in the spirit of inclusive neighbourliness."[7] These populists were interested in community-based direct democracy, with widely heterogeneous populations drawn together by local debate, cooperation and participation. Diverse populations were able to relax and lose their prejudices in the community-supported atmosphere of voluntary civility and respect.

The pluralists had a similar political understanding of community, but saw a far more formal kind of dynamic. For them, "participation was more a requirement than an encouraged product of an open process," and there were a number of competing factions working within the community. The "overall community within the cooperative [was] a negotiated compromise of interests," and

6. Wendell Berry, *Sex, Economy, Freedom and Community* (New York: Pantheon. 1992), p. 14.
7. Allan Heskin, *The Struggle for Community* (Boulder, CO: Westview Press, 1991), p. 40.

WATCH YOURSELF

"the basis of negotiations [was] power, the relative power of the factions, and not the common concerns of the larger group.[8]

The third group, the clientelists, were almost exclusively Latino immigrants. This group sought a "more traditional totalized community of family where blood ties, culture, or ideology is the prime element that holds people together and serves as a cause to exclude the outsider.[9] Clearly different from the pluralists and the populists, this group was interested in homogeneity; consensus reached through private talk and negotiation; obligation to a specifically defined group; and closed, near-impenetrable codes of discourse.

Heskin says that neither the pluralist or clientelist vision is especially safe. Outsiders are shunted aside and "getting in" is difficult, even when significant effort is made. In the Route 2 example, all three conceptions of community, with layers of individualism winding through them, existed together, waxing and waning in popularity and influence. No group was hegemonic, and every issue and debate included threads of all three visions. Heskin spends much of his book looking at patterns of inclusion and exclusion inherent in community discourses: how people decide who gets a voice, and how those decisions are made, challenged and altered. Who gets in and who is shut out is central to thinking about public safety.

John McKnight has also examined patterns of exclusion, particularly within the context of professionalization. In his book *The Careless Society*, McKnight outlines conduits to becoming included in community. He writes that "community is more than just a place. It comprises various groups of people who work together on a face-to-face basis in public life, not just in private."[10]

McKnight's understanding of community is about moving beyond professional management and care, which is ground that Ivan Illich tilled for decades. Through a long series of works, Illich dissected the ways in which professional services disable individuals and communities. He described how traditional, informal (vernacular) life is degraded and displaced by medicalization, education and a culture dominated by professional service. Threading its way throughout Illich's writing is the veneration of self-reliance and the community culture that supports it. This stance is perhaps best articulated in *Medical Nemesis*, where, speaking of pain, he writes:

> *Traditional cultures confront pain, impairment, and death by interpreting them as challenges soliciting a response from the individual under stress;*

8. Ibid., p. 41.
9. Ibid.
10. John McKnight, *The Careless Society* (New York: Basic Books, 1995), p. 118.

medical civilization turns them into demands made by individuals on the economy, into problems that can be managed or produced out of existence. . . . Traditional cultures and technological civilization start from opposite assumptions.[11]

Illich spoke of community as a threatened anomaly within technological civilization, precisely because the possibility of vernacular life is so antithetical to the assumptions upon which professional managers rely. The medicalization of everyday life means the destruction of "the community setting in which suffering can become a dignified performance.[12] Illich's conceptions of community are built on the informal and historical relationships upon which traditional cultures could always rely and which kept them safe.

LOCALITY AND MODERNITY

Identifying the enemies of community is often an easier task than recognizing what distinguishes an understandable vision of community from the infinitely marketable communities that any number of advertisers or cyber-cheerleaders want to pawn off on us. In *Small is Beautiful*, E.F. Schumacher used the word "comprehensible" to describe the appropriate community size.[13] For me, this goes a surprisingly long way toward articulating a place-based rationale. "Comprehensible" inevitably refers to physical, experiential reality, to an understanding that only time and commitment to a place can engender. It's a feel thing.

This is close to what Jane Jacobs was talking about when she described the uses of city neighbourhoods. More than thirty-five years after it was first published, Jacobs' *The Death and Life of Great American Cities* remains among the clearest and sharpest writing about urban space, skipping over dogmatisms and talking about cities from a lived and living perspective. She loves big cities, especially the ones she has lived in (notably New York and Toronto), and doesn't pander to cheap "urban village" formulations. "As a sentimental concept," she says, "'neighbourhood' is harmful to city planning. . . . [and risks] the destruction of a city by converting it into a parcel of towns.[14] Cities are often wonderful, thrilling places to live precisely because of their diversity and the fluid mobility within them. People like cities, and love big cities, for reasons that no village can duplicate, and the reverse is equally true.

I don't want to suggest that cities and community are mutually

11. Ivan Illich, *Medical Nemesis* (New York: Bantam Books, 1976), p. 132.

12. Ibid., p. 116.

13. E.F. Schumacher, *Small is Beautiful* (New York: Harper and Row, 1973).

14. Jane Jacobs, *The Death and Life of Great American Cities* (New York: Vintage, 1992), pp. 112, 115.

WATCH YOURSELF

exclusive or contradictory, but, rather, that thinking about urban and rural neighbourhoods is not a uniform project. Jacobs argues that in thinking about city neighbourhoods, one has to jettison the kinds of small-town, self-contained rationales that apply for smaller places, and acknowledge that a city has an "innate extroversion"[15] and that people like to work, shop, visit, walk and find entertainment all over the city, not only in their neighbourhoods.

Jacobs writes that while a certain percentage of any city's population is fluid, moving around and through various places, every good neighbourhood has to have a base of more or less permanent residents. "If self-government in the place is to work, underlying any float of population must be a continuity of people who have forged neighbourhood networks."[16] If a neighbourhood has that as its base, it can cope with and integrate transient populations.

While it is perilous to speak of city neighbourhoods as "urban villages," there is plenty of room to speak of a connection to land and place as possible and necessary in rural areas, small towns and cities alike. Aldo Leopold is often considered one of the founders of modern ecological and conservationist thinking. A professional forester, he is best known for his posthumous 1949 book *A*

15. Ibid., p. 117.
16. Ibid., p. 138.

Sand County Almanac, in which he outlined "The Land Ethic." He writes that all ethics "rest on a single premise: that the individual is a member of a community of interdependent parts. His instincts prompt him to compete for his place in that community, but his ethics prompt him also to co-operate."[17] Leopold spoke of transforming humanity's place in nature from conqueror to member and citizen by enlarging "the boundaries of the community to include soils, waters, plants, and animals, or collectively, the land."[18]

While a bewildering array of green types continues to claim to be Leopold's legitimate inheritors, Wendell Berry generally makes the most sense to me.[19] Berry has a remarkable capacity to describe community, using ideas like discipline, responsibility, commitment and work in ways that are rarely attempted today. Echoing Leopold, he says:

> *If the word* community *is to mean or amount to anything, it must refer to a place (in its natural integrity) and its people. It must refer to a placed people. Since there obviously can be no cultural relationship that is uniform between a nation and a continent, "community" must mean a people locally placed and a people, moreover, not too numerous to have a common knowledge of themselves and of their place.*[20]

By emphasizing commonality, Berry clearly differentiates

17. Aldo Leopold, *A Sand County Almanac* (New York: Oxford University Press, 1966), p. 219.
18. Ibid.
19. As you've probably guessed by now.
20. Berry, *Sex, Economy, Freedom and Community*, p. 168.

between community and the public. A community necessarily depends on trust, while the public relies on management. Trust is essential to genuine safety. In light of that description, consider the possibilities of online virtual communities[21] where you can't, and are in fact repeatedly warned not to, trust anyone. As the Microsoft ads used to say, there is no race online, there is no gender, there is no disability: it is faceless and placeless. Which returns to Schumacher's "comprehensible" and underlines the assertion that community has to mean local place and include all the relationships within it. As David Schwartz put it, "national community is a contradiction in terms. Community is a local phenomenon."[22]

COME ON IN

Community is nothing if it's not about neighbours and neighbourliness, something not far from what Illich would call "hospitality." Neighbours are drawn together by shared circumstances, by the exigencies of place. The act of living in and caring for a place, any place, is a trying, complex and lengthy one: it is work. Those who are willing to stay put have to contribute time, effort and obligation if a place is to become community. Wendell Berry (again!), relating the words of an Amish farmer:

> At some point, late in the proceedings, they asked David what community meant to him. He said that when he and his son were plowing in the spring he could look around him and see seventeen teams at work on the neighboring farms. He knew those teams and the men driving them, and he knew that if he were hurt or sick, those men and those teams would be at work on his farm.[23]

In his three-part work *The Information Age: Economy, Society and Culture*, Manuel Castells makes an intimidatingly comprehensive attempt to describe current economic and technological transformation, a revolution that "originated and diffused, not by accident, in a historical period of the global restructuring of capitalism, for which it was an essential tool. Thus, the new society emerging from such a process is both capitalist and informational."[24] Part of Castells's analysis is to differentiate and set what he calls "*the space of flows*" — new spatial manifestations of function and power — against "the historically rooted spatial organization of our common experience: *the space of places.*"[25]

In much the same way international capital sloshes funds around

21. See, for a prominent example, Esther Dyson, successful entrepreneur, major player in Internet culture, and daughter of famed physicist Freeman. "There will be — there already is — a profusion of online communities. They are easy to find, and relatively easy to form. But what holds them together? Can a single person in fact be a member of twenty different communities, with each getting his attention fifteen minutes a day (for a total of five hours online)? . . . Thus, a television channel or an Internet 'channel' can create or reflect a culture, but in order for it to become a community its members have to communicate with one another — ideally in the context of some goal. That goal may only

the globe, always searching for profit and easy markets, information and power are now sloshing around in this space of flows where "[localities] become disembodied from their cultural, historical, geographic meaning, and reintegrated into functional networks, or into image collages, inducing a space of flows that substitutes for the space of places."[26] People, however, still live in places and derive comprehensible meaning from and through their places, and thus "[experience], by being related to places, becomes abstracted from power, and meaning is increasingly separated from knowledge. It follows a structural schizophrenia between two spatial logics."[27]

What Castells is identifying here is a kind of contemporary confusion, so noticeable when entering an online community, a "place" where everything shifts, nothing can be taken for granted and all the touchstone evocations of neighbourly warmth are up for grabs, yet the language and signs are familiar. In Castells's space of flows, only the global elite has any ability to move freely, to negotiate the structural schizophrenia to its advantage. "Thus, CMC [computer mediated communication] may be a powerful medium to reinforce the social cohesion of the cosmopolitan elite, providing material support to the meaning of a global culture."[28] This global culture is necessarily at odds with local places, not only culturally, but also physically and historically.

COMMUNITY SIMULACRA

Like no other tools before, information technologies have arrived with a veritable avalanche of marketing, advertising and sheer hype. Much of this has tapped into a public more than willing to listen to, and buy into, claims of community and communication. As Stephen Talbott writes,

> *The obvious lie should already have alerted us to the dangers. A culture that has largely succeeded in eradicating the last traces of its own village life turns around and — by appealing to a yet further extension of the eradicating technology — encourages itself with Edenic images of a global village. This is Doublespeak. The television, having helped to barricade the villager behind the walls of his own home, will not now convert the world into a village simply by enabling him to watch the bombs falling on Baghdad. Nor will we suddenly be delivered from ourselves by making television interactive and investing it with computing power. . . . Nor do we see evidence of escape from the inexorable, despotic logic already responsible for the fortification and isolation of our own inner-city "villages."[29]*

be homage to a star, but it could also be political action, a business plan, or a school. A community is a shared asset, created by the investment of its members." Esther Dyson, *Release 2.0* (New York: Broadway, 1997), pp. 32–33.

22. David Schwartz, *Who Cares?* (Boulder, CO: Westview Press, 1997), p. 45.

23. Wendell Berry, *Home Economics* (San Francisco: North Point, 1987), p. 188.

24. Manuel Castells, *The Rise of the Network Society* (Malden, MA: Blackwell, 1996), p. 13.

25. Ibid., p. 378.

26. Ibid., p. 375.

27. Ibid., p. 428.

28. Ibid., p. 364.

29. Stephen L. Talbott, *The Future Does Not Compute* (Sebastopol, CA: O'Reilly and Associates, 1995), p. 113.

The idea that global interconnectivity is laying the groundwork for actual community is gibberish: virtual relationships are only vaguely and trivially akin to face-to-face relationships. As John Gray put it in the *Manchester Guardian*, the Internet is "a designer Utopia customised for people who believe in technical fixes and not in morality or politics and the long haul we face in the struggle to protect our human and natural environments."[30]

Sometimes when you raise questions about new technologies you get called a Luddite, which ain't so bad in my book. Luddites were cottage workers in the middle counties of England who rose up in 1811 and 1812 against the imposition of textile machinery, which was obliterating their community culture and livelihoods. In their public letter of March 1812 they wrote that they were not opposed to all machinery but to "all Machinery hurtful to Commonality,"[31] a brilliant phrase, I think, in the midst of a techno tsunami. The Luddite argument was never only about technology; it was about local power and control. The languages of globalization are fundamentally at odds with the health of local languages and community culture. If we are going to rethink safety, it has to be in the context of community, and we have to know what we are talking about.

30. John Gray, "Cyberspace Offers a Hollow Freedom," *Manchester Guardian*, April 16, 1995.

31. Quoted in Kirkpatrick Sale, *Rebels Against the Future* (Reading, MA: Addison-Wesley, 1995), p. 261.

CHAPTER FIVE

Getting Back to Nature:

Adventure Operators

Are Standing By

If human beings once knew what "nature" was, they do so no longer.
ULRICH BECK, ANTHONY GIDDENS AND SCOTT LASH,
Reflexive Modernization

Nature is perhaps the most complex word in the language.
RAYMOND WILLIAMS, *Keywords*

The fall of 2005 left a lot of people wondering about the natural world. Still reeling fom the previous December's Asian tsunami, and with the Bush administration's grudging concession that maybe humans have something to do with global warming came hurricane season. Katrina's brutal treatment of the Gulf Coast and New Orleans exposed a tangible and often explicit uncertainty: the implication was that this hurricane was a harbinger of future catastrophes. That a whole city could be drowned undermined a certain sense of control. That "Mother Nature" could be so callous had people feeling fatalistic and bitter.

In a lot of ways, our base notions of safety are deeply rooted in our relationship with what we call "nature." It is useful to trace our weird cultural contortions as we try to make sense of our place in the natural world and decide what is "natural," because I think they can illuminate what we want to mean by *safe*.

A nice starting point is camping. Most of us have a certain expectation of "getting back to nature" when we go camping, that we will interact with the natural world in a way that is supposed to be good for us: honest, simple, basic, virtuous. We want and expect varying degrees of this: some want a very komfortable kampsite with showers, kamp programming and kamp amenities. Others like more of a rough-and-tumble experience with informal sites, no bathrooms and few rules. Both have very specific degrees of intersection that they are hoping for and will go a long way to get.

The komfy kampers bring an RV and most of their belongings; the more adventurous types drive a long way down a logging road and 4x4 into an isolated forest site. Both are defining and limiting what they want, constructing the experience on their terms and human expectations.

I understand this, and still my long-held prejudices get in the way easily. As a child backpacking with my family, I learned early that anyone who carried too much stuff with them wasn't really camping, not like us. My dad openly considered anyone who brought even a flashlight a pussy and a blight on the wilderness. I have the same reaction when I bring tarps with me; there's just something about stringing up a bunch of blue plastic that makes me feel like I'm cheating.

I know this makes no sense: I have more or less arbitrarily decided what makes for an "authentic" camping experience, and judge anyone who looks for more comfort as somehow inadequate. It's the same thing when I drive into an isolated site somewhere and there are other people there. I get pissy, as if they are infringing on my nature experience. We all want just the right amount of adventure — no more, no less — but the reality is that camping is only the simulacra of adventure. It's not very adventurous if we design it beforehand. How much komfort one likes is an aesthetic argument, but it is one that gets cloaked in the language of virtue.

It is both unsettling and comforting to drive into an isolated

WATCH YOURSELF

campsite and see a forty-eight–foot RV named *Wilderness* resting in an adjacent site. There can be no question that the hulking giant shatters certain illusions, but the possibility of catching a football game on its satellite dish offers a level of relief. On a more prosaic level, if anything were to happen, an emergency or something, civilization sits a few metres away, and the droning backbeat of potential ambiguity is muted.

I think there is reason to consider RVs, not only because there are so damn many of them, but because their ubiquity reveals something a little more textured. To speak of safety is to speak of ironing out danger and uncertainty, and to use that as a historically (and ontologically) placed good is to rely on specific renditions of nature our culture holds dear.

Put another way, when we think of safety, we essentially want to move both to and from nature: toward the gentle embrace of Mother Nature and away from the capricious, uncontrolled and destructive nature that brings us tsunamis and hurricanes and drought. Unfortunately, it's pretty hard to have it both ways, and paying attention to that conundrum takes us some way toward figuring out what we could and should mean by *safe*.

△

If it is true that the West no longer knows what "nature" is, it is equally true that popular discourses tend to rebound ferociously between not caring all that much and caring way too much. Considering what we mean when we speak of nature is a slippery question, one that is more interesting and more important than it seems at first glance, and the answer has everyday implications for our thinking about safety, public life and the nature (!) of culture.

In an era of profound ecological degradation, it is worth looking at how, where and why we name some things "natural" and others not. The core thrust of mainstream environmentalism, for example, is about *human* safety in a polluted and increasingly toxic world, and yet, as Mark Roseland has written:

> The very concept of "environmental protection" is based on the separation of humanity from nature. As a society, we point to a few things we think of as nature — some trees here, a pond there — draw a circle around them, and then try to "protect" what's within the circle. Meanwhile, we ignore the fact that human activity outside that circle — housing, economic development, transportation, and so on — has a far greater impact on the environment than do our "environmental" policies.[1]

1. Mark Roseland, "Ecological Planning for Sustainable Communities," in *Futures by Design*, Doug Aberley, ed. (Gabriola Island, BC: New Society, 1994), p. 71.

Whether humanity resides within nature, beside it or above it is central to ecological thinking, and a certain scepticism about "nature" constructions is essential.

In part, I contend that most of our contemporary perceptions of safeness are organized around nature as Otherness — an inherently unpredictable Otherness. The separation is critical for placing ourselves and our protection in an antagonistic tension with whatever our culture feels like naming "natural."

Like everything else in late-capitalist culture, the idea of nature is full of back doors, contradictions and detours. Western notions of nature and the wilderness have been documented well and thoroughly in recent academic and popular writing, but what we are left with is a complicated and complicating question.

How we perceive nature and "the wild" has plenty to do with how we grasp the trajectories of safety and how we culturally conceive of public and private policy making. That is, the ideal of safety lies at the heart of our conceptions of the good life, and that ideal is guided largely by how we construct our relationships with nature and wildness. Whether it is nature within or without, our inner beast or the wild forest, nature and safeness are consistently placed in antipathy to one another, just as the biological world (first nature) and the human social world (second nature) are so often positioned as antagonistic.[2]

2. I draw frequently in this chapter on Murray Bookchin's dialectical naturalism. Nature philosophy runs throughout his writings, maybe most accessibly in *Toward an Ecological Society* (Montreal: Black Rose, 1980); *Remaking Society* (Montreal: Black Rose, 1989); *The Philosophy of Social Ecology* (Montreal: Black Rose, 1995).

WILDING

There is no wilderness left. To speak of wilderness is to speak of the opposite of culture, the opposite of human control, and there are few spots anywhere in the world that have not been mapped, surveyed, photographed, explored, hunted, mined, logged, examined and evaluated by modern humans. Actually, there are none. Where there is no human settlement there is resource extraction, tourism, Google Earth, satellite tracking, scientific exploration, a military presence or at least monitoring, and the threat of looming development.

More importantly, dualistic interpretations of wilderness rarely acknowledge the shifting constructions of the idea itself and the social soil from which wilderness emerges. As William Cronon writes:

The removal of Indians to create "uninhabited wilderness" — uninhabited as never before in the human history of the place — reminds us just

how invented, just how constructed, the American wilderness really is. To return to my opening argument: there is nothing natural about the concept of wilderness. It is entirely a creation of the culture that holds it dear, a product of the very history it seeks to deny. . . .

To this day, for instance, the Blackfeet continue to be accused of "poaching" on the lands of Glacier National Park that originally belonged to them and that were ceded by treaty only with the proviso that they be permitted to hunt there.[3]

3. William Cronon, "The Trouble With Wilderness; or, Getting Back to the Wrong Nature," in *Uncommon Ground: Toward Reinventing Nature*, William Cronan, ed. (New York: Norton, 1996), p. 79.

That is not to say there is not still mystery or *wildness* left in the world. In any forest or canyon or bay there are still infinite pieces of the natural world existing and thriving that humans do not, and perhaps cannot, understand or measure. There are innumerable parts of the world, forlorn and empty, that are largely unknown, but the difference between wildness and wilderness is a significant one. The wild and mysterious parts of the world are that way still because we let them be.

This is a stance that overwhelmingly places the fate of the earth in human hands: frankly a grim and regrettable position. I do not believe that humans reside at the pinnacle of natural evolution; I do not believe that humans represent any kind of biotic climax, nor do I believe that human language justifies natural domination in the name of our own safety and protection. I do believe, however, that we find in ourselves a unique product of evolution, armed with a self-consciousness elsewhere unavailable. Humans are certainly left holding the fate of the earth in our grubby little hands, and the decisions about what does and doesn't constitute nature, and whether we stand within or outside nature, are critical quandaries that are at the core of ecological thinking.

To the extent that we celebrate wilderness as the measure with which we judge civilization, we reproduce the dualism that sets humanity and nature at opposite poles. We thereby leave ourselves little hope of discovering what an ethical, sustainable, honourable human place in nature might look like.[4]

△

In her 1980 book *The Death of Nature*, Carolyn Merchant articulated an eco-feminist stance, claiming that in organic societies, nature has always been perceived as female.[5] She suggested that, after the Scientific Revolution, a mechanistic world view based in male, mathematical analysis reduced and conflated both women and nature, often violently and always with the intent to control and manage.

The female earth was central to the organic cosmology that was undermined by the Scientific Revolution and the rise of a market-oriented culture in early modern Europe. . . . when our cosmos ceased to be viewed as an organism and became instead a machine. . . .

We must re-examine the formation of a world-view and a science that, by reconceptualizing reality as a machine rather than a living organism, sanctioned the domination of both nature and women.[6]

Through to the 1600s, Merchant says, nature was regarded as nurturing, and Mother Earth was unambiguously female. The European world view, articulated by Greek and Roman philosophers through to Descartes, Newton, Shakespeare and Milton, dominantly viewed nature as organic: passive, giving and caring. Incursions such as mining were usually regarded as infused with avarice and violence toward a matronly earth. The Scientific Revolution, which Merchant dates as occurring between 1500 and 1700, gradu-

4. Ibid., p. 81.
5. Merchant continues to exert a surprising pull on contemporary ecological notions, and while some of her analysis now seems dated, in part that is because her work has been so thoroughly integrated into contemporary feminist, ecological and environmental conversations.
6. Carolyn Merchant, *The Death of Nature* (San Francisco: Harper and Row, 1983), pp. xx–xxi.

ally and incrementally overwhelmed this cosmology and displaced female, organic nature with a mechanistic view.

Through these two centuries, Merchant argues, nature began to be seen as "a disorderly and chaotic realm to be subdued and controlled."[7] It was recast as an untrustworthy and volatile beast that could be peaceful, pastoral and welcoming one minute; wild, violent and destructive the next. The view of women, so long closely associated with nature, became similarly dualistic: women were virginal, motherly and caring or vicious, witchish and unpredictable. Both needed to be managed and carefully monitored, and a scientific world view emerged that saw man's highest and clearest purpose as the defeat and dominion of the natural world. Careful observation of natural phenomena, experimentation and technical innovation — the Scientific Method — became a mantra for an era. Bacon instructed men of science that nature must be "bound into service" and made a "slave," put "in constraint" and "moulded" by mechanical arts.[8]

Part of *The Death of Nature's* enduring importance is that Merchant recognized the impact of the Scientific Method's fixation on minute observation and prediction. Contemporary culture remains obsessed with removing the guesswork from interactions with nature. The glut of media-porn about the Asian tsunami in December 2004 made this evident at a whole new level. The quake and wave were characterized as unpredictable, capricious and impetuous, while disaster response teams and weather forecasters armed with satellite tracking devices and 3-D predictive computer software bravely attempted to predict and protect.

While many of us want to experience "nature," through camping or otherwise, not so many are interested in dispensing with the possibility of calling 911 on a moment's notice. I want to believe that I am out there in nature, communing with it and conquering it, but really only to a certain extent. And that extent is governed by my aesthetic resistance to tarps and flashlights, my desire to pretend to be tough, and whatever urges for authenticity might be propelling me.

THE DESIRE TO CONTROL DESIRE

In 2000, a pair of teens snowboarded out of bounds on a major ski hill here in Vancouver and fell to their deaths. The hill was double- and triple-roped off, signs were posted and brochures were handed out, but the girls ignored the warnings, ducked under the ropes and

7. Ibid., p. 127.
8. Ibid., p. 169.

boarded the backcountry, with disastrous results. In the aftermath, the story took another turn when the girls' families spoke publicly of responsibility and safeness:

9. *Vancouver Sun*, March 28, 2000, p. A1.

The tragedy has shaken the Jalali and Emami families, as well as their friends at West Vancouver Secondary, where Shekoo was in Grade 10 and Tara in Grade 11.

Saied Jalali, Shekoo's father, said the buddies took beginner snowboarding lessons in December, and hit the slopes together twice a week this winter.

He said the girls were becoming accomplished riders, and questioned whether the ropes and signs at Cypress were proper deterrents to keep youngsters out of the backcountry.

"We would appreciate if somebody would explain to us and let us know if all the major safety measures were done," the grieving father said.

Added his brother John Jalali: "There should have been more security, and barriers and fences for the treacherous ravine and the creek that is over there. We feel someone is responsible for this great loss. We want to make sure that Cypress management in the future prevents these kinds of tragedies."[9]

WATCH YOURSELF

I have no interest in critiquing the comments of a grieving family, but what I find interesting is that these kinds of questions immediately surface in the wake of any human injury or property loss. Who is responsible? Did the authorities do enough? Was safety institutionalized?

The short but keen debate that followed in the letters section of the paper predictably and perhaps appropriately revolved around personal responsibility and the attribution of private blame, but the constant was incredulous and morbid fixation on the vagaries of nature. Not just that wild nature, even on the roped, signed, supervised, mapped, tracked and monitored ski hill could be so alive and dangerous, but that inner nature could be so capricious. As a fellow student said, "I don't know why they did that. They were smart and mature girls." Another underlined the point, "They shouldn't have done it because there are big signs that say don't go there. They think they can do it, but they can't."[10]

There is something more here than simple good idea/bad idea kinds of instrumental analysis. There is a territory here where first (biological) nature and second (human) nature speak, where desire becomes social and nature becomes culture. Whether humans are ignoring grim warnings on cigarette packs or out-of-bounds ropes on ski hills, the desire for transgression, for adventure, for desire, is not so easily passed off as a moment of stupidity. Isabelle Stengers says that "life is an adventure, and indeed some adventures have a bad end, but the end is not the moral of the adventure."[11] The truly dangerous tendency, in my estimation, is the urge to make all of first nature — human or otherwise — the Other. The infinite gradations of authority, of maintenance and of control are a perilous place to start reconceptualizing the tension between first and second nature, between culture and nature. It is all too easy to conflate nature with risk as an ill-defined Otherness, as a looming antagonist that exists independently of circumstance.

Western relationships with nature are rife with postmodern contradictions, like hiking while clutching a cell phone, or all those ads for monster GPS-laden SUVs, marketed for back-to-the-land, adventurous guys. The environmental movements of the past forty years have had a significant impact on recasting policy around, and perceptions of, nature, but at the heart of our economic and social life lies a certain profound and layered distrust of the natural world.

It is a discourse most of us are familiar with. Our culture wants to preserve at least a *simulacra* of nature, to control it as if it were a creature in a zoo, extracting the simulated wild experience while never straying far from safeness.

10. Ibid.
11. Isabelle Stengers, "A Cosmo-Politics: Risk, Hope, Change," in *Hope: New Philosophies for Change*, Mary Zournazi, ed. (New York: Routledge, 2002), pp. 249–50.

STAY OFF THE GRASS

12. Raymond Williams, *Keywords* (London: Fontana, 1976), p. 219.

It is difficult to grasp, even on reflection, what is actually meant in either official or vernacular discourses by "nature."

It is relatively easy to distinguish three areas of meaning: (i) the essential quality and character of something; (ii) the inherent force which directs either the world or human beings or both; (iii) the material world itself, taken as including or not including human beings. Yet it is evident that within (ii) and (iii), though the area of reference is broadly clear, precise meanings are variable and at times even opposed. The historical development of the word through these three senses is important, but it is also significant that all three senses, and the main variations and alternatives within the two most difficult of them, are still active and widespread in contemporary usage.[12]

Ideas of nature, the natural world and wilderness are often conflated to mean more or less the same things, and they are contrasted with the human world. The ideas, and uses of the ideas, are constantly contradictory and often infused with irony. A tree is usually described as "nature" whether it is in a forest or a city park. But if that tree is put in a pot and planted in a back garden it becomes something else. A patch of grass is definitely nature when it is in a meadow in the countryside, but it's not quite the same when it is a field for goats to graze and is certainly different when it is used as a playing surface in a football stadium.

We are as easily confused about animals as plants. A wolf is "natural"; a dog, not really, but it has a "wild" instinct. Horses are wild and part of nature when they are running on Sable Island, but less so when they are ponies ridden at a country fair. Wolves and elephants and snakes are "wild animals," while guinea pigs and goldfish are always something else again. Cats are hardly wild when curled on a lap, but their natural instinct emerges when they kill a bird. And that's not even going near Dolly the Cloned Sheep.

Wild nature is unpredictable and dangerous, while domesticated natural beings are safe and controlled. Humans too, despite posing as the antithesis of nature, are regarded as having dangerous "natural impulses," somehow different and separate from cultural or conscious urges. Both good and evil elements of human activities are variously ascribed to nature.

Historically, "nature" has meant deep, inherent tendencies, either in plants, animals or humans. It can refer to innate characteristics

WATCH YOURSELF

and the forces that caused movements and developments in the world. Almost always, nature is contrasted with the made, that which humans have built: culture. It is worth asking to what extent the idea of nature itself is constructed, for the uses of "nature" have been many, often reactionary, oppressive and disgraceful. I think it is useful to be suspicious of "nature" and to ask where and how humans have constructed it.

At every step, how we view nature is a cultural question. As Alexander Wilson put it,

Nature is a part of culture. When our physical surroundings are sold to us as "natural" (like the travel ad for "Super, Natural, British Columbia") we should pay close attention. Our experience of the natural world — whether touring the Canadian Rockies, watching an animal show on TV, or working in our own gardens — is always mediated. It is always shaped by rhetorical constructs like photography, industry, advertising, and aesthetics, as well as by institutions like religion, tourism and education.[13]

So are humans inside or outside nature? It is arguable that premodern cultures tended to view humans as largely indistinguishable from the biotic and animal life around them, residing within a web of natural life. If this were so, a different world view began to take shape with the rise of logocentric Greek thinking and the emergence of monotheism.

What was radical in both Hebrew and early Christian thought was its profound anthropocentrism and its abandonment of a cyclical for a linear conception of time. Hellenism and Judeo-Christianity in combination introduced an unprecedented direction to human intercourse with the earth, for nature was conceived as valueless until humanized.[14]

13. Alexander Wilson, *The Culture of Nature* (Toronto: Between the Lines, 1991), p. 12.

14. Max Oelschlaeger, *The Idea of Wilderness* (New Haven, CT: Yale University Press, 1991), p. 33. Italics in original.

15. Cited in Oelschlaeger, *The Idea of Wilderness*, p. 43.

This shift in thinking underlies most modern conceptions of nature, a view of humanity standing outside and above nature.

Certainly much contemporary ecological and environmental thought points to this Judeo-Christian tradition. As Lynn White says, "We shall continue to have a worsening ecologic crisis until we reject the Christian axiom that nature has no reason for existence except to serve man."[15] The vernacular understanding of the Biblical imperative is that the land and its plants and creatures were given to man to have dominion over. The interpretive and etymological meanings of dominion and stewardship are of deep interest to those of a Biblical bent, but there can be little doubt that "dominion" has been central to forging Western conceptions of nature.

At the heart of speaking about nature are conceptions of good and evil. For certain and specific reasons, nature is often evoked as the wellspring of all that is good. The trees, the streams, the mountains, the birds, the animals, the children are seen as just and innocent, holding within them virtue crystallized. The idea is a widely held and familiar one, perhaps articulated most clearly by Romantic poets, like William Wordsworth in "The Tables Turned":

> Come forth into the light of things,
> Let Nature be your Teacher.
>
> She has a world of ready wealth,
> Our minds and hearts to bless—
> Spontaneous wisdom breathed by health,
> Truth breathed by cheerfulness.
>
> One impulse from a vernal wood
> May teach you more of man,
> Of moral evil and of good,
> Than all the sages can.[16]

This Romantic sentiment for nature is maintained by writers such as Thoreau — "Our village life would stagnate if it were not for the

16. William Wordsworth, "The Tables Turned." *Norton Anthology of English Literature*, Vol. 2 (New York: Norton, 1968), p. 94.

WATCH YOURSELF

unexplored forests and meadows which surround it. We need the tonic of wildness.... We can never have enough of Nature"[17] — and more recent wilderness defenders like Edward Abbey: "The planet will be a better place when most of us are gone."[18]

The idealization of nature as "the greatest teacher of all" is an entrenched and widely referenced one and in many ways suggests a humanity that is not *part* of nature, but is above or perhaps beside or beneath it. It is a distinction that has worked from Aristotle on and was further defined by Descartes, who argued that "animals, deprived of a soul, are in effect no more sentient than plants, and therefore lack the capacity of feeling pleasure and pain in any subjective sense."[19]

Turning nature into an objectified *thing*, be it deity or resource, is critical for maintaining separation of the human and natural worlds, and for ignoring first and second nature continuity. Denying nature's subjectivity has layers of implication:

> The history of "civilization" has been a steady process of estrangement
> from nature that has increasingly developed into outright antagonism....
> We slander the natural world when we deny its activity, striving, creativity,
> and development as well as its subjectivity. Nature is never drugged. Our
> re-entry into natural evolution is no less a humanization of nature than a
> naturalization of humanity.[20]

When we fixate on human separation from the natural world, we play into fearful notions of wildness, the idea that the natural world, both within us and around us, is capricious and dangerous, very likely out to get us.

UNNATURAL NATURE

Importantly, Western views of nature that subsume trees and plants and rocks and mountains and animals also tend to subsume "natives." From the first European incursions into New Worlds, the peoples living there have always been regarded as part of the wilderness landscapes, part of the natural world to be worked around, with or, most usually, through, depending on exigency and efficacy. Equally pervasive within the "noble savage" tradition is the mythologizing of Indians as living in perfect ecological harmony, thus denying them humanity and iconicizing them along with the natural world.[21]

Too often the idea of safety relies heavily on the Otherness of

17. Henry David Thoreau, *The Variorum Walden*, annotated and with an introduction by Walter Harding (NewYork: Twayne, 1962), p. 255.

18. Edward Abbey, "Edward Abbey Interviews Himself," *Whole Earth Review*, no. 61, Winter 1988, p. 17.

19. Quoted in Kate Soper, *What Is Nature?* (Oxford: Blackwell, 1995), p. 53.

20. Murray Bookchin, *The Ecology of Freedom* (Palo Alto, CA: Cheshire, 1982), p. 315.

the natural world and the absence of natural subjectivity, leaving culture as indisputably "ours." Safeness means creating a comfort zone between culture and nature, a freedom *from* a nature we reside above or at least are breaking from.

Western (Conradian even) eagerness to view the natural world and the non-Western world as the Other means we are compelled to take advantage of available landscapes/resources. At the heart of the development of new technologies has always been what Frederick Turner called the West's "long push outward,"[22] the attempt to quell nature, make it ours, civilize it. Much of this attempt is shrouded by mythology and informed by fear. Whether it is animals, bad weather, time, distance, death or food, technology is driven by second nature's antagonism and transcendent aspirations. It is almost impossible to talk about nature without thinking about technology. If culture is posed as the antithesis of nature, than technology is the set of tools culture uses to assert itself against the natural world.[23] The dialectical relationship between safeness and our long push outward is one that even a casual observer of the social construction of nature cannot avoid.

21. For the best exploration of this attitude see Shepard Krech, *The Ecological Indian* (New York: Norton, 1999).

22. Frederick Turner, *Beyond Geography* (New York: Viking, 1980), p. 6.

23. See Chapter Eight for more on this.

△

What I am offering here is an admittedly cursory consideration of nature. The question of nature is a vast and tentacled one that keeps reaching out further and further, but asking the question has real value (if only heuristically). I do believe that how our culture considers the natural, and how the queries are voiced, is key to piecing together the genealogy of safeness, to figuring out how we can reasonably and honourably talk about safety.

To say that our cultural heritage considers humanity as standing outside nature, and views wilderness as an Otherness, is only a particular kind of truth. There are those who argue for humans to explicitly place themselves within nature, not as a middling entity in the Chain of Being, but as another piece of the ecological web. I am sincerely attracted to much of this thinking, but as Kate Soper writes:

> *In its commonest and most fundamental sense, the term "nature" refers to everything which is not human and distinguished from the work of humanity. . . . I speak of this conception of "otherness" to humanity as fundamental because, although many would question whether or not we can in fact draw any such rigid divide, the conceptual distinction remains indispensable. Whether, for example, it is claimed that "nature" and*

"culture" are clearly differentiated realms or that no hard and fast delinea-
tion can be made between them, all such thinking is tacitly reliant on the
nature-humanity antithesis itself. . . .

It is correct to insist that "nature" is the idea through which we concep-
tualize what is "other" to ourselves.[24]

I think that Soper has it essentially correct in that last line. To
move from there to a genuinely ecological stance that can face and
include Otherness, the constructed qualities of nature, and manage
to conceive of a humanity that is not compelled to dominate nature
— a humanity that places itself simultaneously within and separate from nature and is reconciled to that place — is no joke, but
possible.

As Max Oelschlaeger asks, "Dare we think that we are nature
watching nature?"[25] Sure, but that still doesn't let us off the hook.
Humans are something else again, or as Terry Eagleton has it (beau-
tifully), "Human nature is naturally unnatural, overflowing the
measure simply by virtue of what it is. . . . it is just part of the way
we are constructed, that demand should outstrip need, that culture
should be of our nature."[26]

I want this chapter to point to some Western ideas about nature
and control, because that is the soil from which our conversations
about safety grow. Our culture is swamped with identifications of
the Other and subsequent idealization, irony, vilification, pater-
nalism, antagonism, romanticism and domination. We inherit
three millennia of civilization clutching the idea of controlling the
Other, and nature, whether within or without, tends to get reduced
to the big Other.

Our compulsion toward safeness is an expression of this dominant cultural impulse writ both small and global. I am interested
in second nature's suspicion and hostility toward first nature, in all
its formulations, and how that suspicion is reconfigured as instinc-
tual virtue. Increasing the separation between culture and nature
and mediating the relationship between first and second nature is
fundamentally what is meant by safety and what is then passed off
as an *a priori*, apolitical good.

24. Soper, *What is
Nature?*, pp. 16–17.

25. Oelschlaeger,
*The Idea of Wilder-
ness*, p. 350.

26. Terry Eagle-
ton, *The Idea of
Culture* (Oxford:
Blackwell, 2000),
p. 18.

Safe School Planning Guide

BRITISH COLUMBIA

Ministry of Attorney General Ministry of Education
Working Together for Safe Schools and Safe Communities

CHAPTER SIX

Don't Even Think About Bringing That in Here

Schooling for Safety

I kept making the same mistake, and it was a serious one: I kept wanting to teach. I wanted our school to be more relevant to the needs of the boys. And they, of course, kept throwing me off. What they needed, and obviously craved, was a dose of the big world.

GEORGE DENNISON, THE LIVES OF CHILDREN:
The Story of the First Street School

Two institutions at present control our children's lives: television and schooling, in that order. Both of these reduce the real world of wisdom, fortitude, temperance and justice to a never-ending, non-stop abstraction. . . . I've noticed a fascinating phenomenon in my twenty-five years of teaching: that schools and schooling are increasingly irrelevant to the great enterprises of the planet. . . . Schools are intended to produce, through the application of formulas, formulaic human beings whose behaviour can be predicted and controlled.

JOHN GATTO, *Dumbing Us Down*

The new world of safety and security consciousness has affected every workplace in varying ways, many of which can be considered exercises in *governmentality*. It's a term and an idea with Foucauldian origins[1] that draws on the same historiography as some of Ian Hacking's work,[2] and it refers to the management and regulation of "populations" based on statistical information gathering. Using the flood of data at their disposal, experts now make calculations based on the normalization of populations to predict and control patterns of behaviour and regulate groups of people.

Information about diverse risks is collected and analysed by medical researchers, statisticians, sociologists, demographers, environmental scientists, legal practitioners, bankers and accountants, to name a few. Through these never-ceasing efforts, particular social groups or popula-

1. See Graham Burchell, Colin Gordon and Peter Miller, eds., *The Foucault Effect: Studies in Governmentality* (Hemel Hempstead, UK: Harvester Wheatsheaf, 1991).

2. See my discussions of Hacking in Chapters One and Ten.

tions are identified as "at-risk" or "high-risk", requiring particular forms of knowledges and interventions.[3]

Thus risk becomes a moral question. If people do not take calculated expert advice on how to care for themselves or how to behave, they are deemed irresponsible, negligent or morally lax by putting themselves in "danger." This kind of discourse is common in so many workplaces: emergency procedures posted on doors, admonitions to employees to wash their hands, directives about what kind of work boots you have to wear, insurance requirements, rules setting out what you are and are not allowed to do at work. I find this language kind of poignant because I work mostly with kids that others would call "at-risk" or "high-risk," kids who are identified as needing expert intervention and who are familiar with having their situations described (by themselves as often as professionals) as beyond their control.

△

I'm sitting here at my desk, staring at a pink box. It's a government-issue workbox, maybe a foot cubed, brightly coloured and labelled "Safe Schools Kit," and it's full of documents that came to the school I once worked at — pamphlets, posters, stickers, directives, planning guides and legal folders. It has always proved good reading for me, and over the past four or five years I have been cutting out and adding to it any useful newspaper, journal or magazine articles I come across that relate to safety. As you might imagine, there is a hefty pile of clippings. As I sit here and fish them out, organizing them in categories, I am amazed at how many are about schools.

The volume of school stories speaks to my personal predilections, as I have always been interested in compulsory schooling. I also think it indicates the degree to which our cultural fixation with safety focuses most intensely on children.

Many parents justify otherwise incomprehensible behaviours with "It's for the children" rationales: moving to the suburbs, buying a minivan, forgetting dreams, getting serious, etc. Children are a catch-all excuse for innumerable strange decisions, and people often force kids to abide by restrictions and mandates that make little sense except to appease our own neuroses. Many aspects of schools are the most flagrant by-products of these kinds of rationales, as children are required to adhere to constant regulation, surveillance, monitoring, authority, and punishment.[4] For most schools, the increasing impossibility of their mandates means they

3. Deborah Lupton, *Risk* (London: Routledge, 1999), p. 87.

4. Consider having to ask to go to the bathroom, getting punished for talking out of turn to colleagues, changing rooms at the sound of a bell, eating only when allowed, negotiating security guards roaming the halls, being surveilled and assessed constantly. These are just a quick litany of normative school realities. They are also the daily realities in too many jobsites: schools both reflect and construct larger, adult social realities. Schools prepare students for the "real world" and help build it.

have to continually retreat into policies of control.

Each clipping I pull out of the box is more fun then the previous one: Blair Okays School Drug Testing.[5] Unruly Students Facing Arrest, Not Detention,[6] Nervous High Schools Begin Putting ID Tags on Students,[7] and most recently a story about a five-year-old arrested and cuffed for bad kindergarten behaviour.[8] I'll stop now, but there is story after story like this. Throwing students in the can for being noisy? Putting tags on them like dogs? Random, mandatory drug testing? Arresting a five-year-old? What is this?

I recognize the sensationalism here, but I submit that these measures, like now less-headline-friendly ones (security guards roaming schools, random locker searches with drug-sniffing dogs, metal detectors at the doors), are the necessary and logical outcomes of the schooled impulse. In B.C., for example, many schools have now implemented "smart card" tracking technology that allows schools and parents to track their kids throughout the day, monitor their cafeteria purchases and find out whether they were late and when they left school.

> The program, called FirstStudent™ Solution[9] . . . will have four components. . . . The first component will enable students to use their student cards as debit cards in the cafeteria. The second is an asset management program that tracks school equipment, such as textbooks or musical instruments, that have been loaned to the student. The third lets parents pay online for school fees, such as field trips. And the fourth tracks a student's attendance, including tardiness and skipping classes.
>
> All the information will be kept in a database that is accessible by parents via the Internet. . . .
>
> Right now, every school in the country has an information system that tracks students, teachers and classes and many have attendance systems built in, Woods said. But with FirstStudent, parents have "real-time hook-up," which enables them to log on and see if their child was late or checked out of school for any reason.[10]

This chapter could easily head off in any number of different directions, so I am going to limit it to a couple of specific points. I won't talk about emotional safety, bullying or the widespread use of biopsychiatric drugs. And I won't tell the story of Alberta teachers forbidden to speak about vegetarianism due to fears for their farm students' emotional safety. Promise, I'll leave that story alone. All these have clear and relevant bearing on the discussion but will have to wait for another day.

5. "Schools will have the ability to carry out random drug testing on students .... [British prime minister Tony] Blair said school principals will have the right to either offer treatment to children caught by the tests, expel them or report them to police." *Vancouver Sun*, February 21, 2004.

6. A girl in Toledo, Ohio, refused to change a low-cut shirt, even after her mother was called, in violation of her school's dress code. She was handcuffed and jailed briefly.

CURRICULUMS FROM WAL-MART

First, I want to point out the degree to which schools and places that deal with kids[11] have been forced to strictly limit their range of activities, and how safety-rationalized calculations have forced schools into becoming ever more standardized and monocultural. Small schools, alternative programs, experience-based schools — all of these have a hell of a time springing up and maintaining their programs, in part because of the restrictions imposed by insurance providers, building codes, safety inspectors and school boards.

One of the functional realities of Wal-Mart economics is that almost everything is cheaper when you buy it in bulk. That is clear to anyone who has ever bought laundry detergent or toilet paper. In terms of insurance, size or numbers have extra importance when considering assets, risk and coverage. Smaller projects and institutions are burdened by their lack of collateral assets when they ask insurance providers to provide coverage: the bigger an organization, the more likely it is to get a reasonable price. Small schools and clubs have to affiliate themselves with larger bodies or pay extra premiums to make up for their lack of organizational assets. The smaller the group, the bigger the insurance risk.

Insurance is right in front of any school that is interested in providing outside-the-classroom experience and is always an issue when kids are on the premises. Organizations have to be able to cover themselves in terms of liability. Smaller, more adventurous schools get financially squeezed, and the encouragement to get big is overt and conspicuous, forcing many programs to become more standardized, less innovative, more regulated.

There are several quality ski hills surrounding Vancouver, and every winter there are numerous school ski trips. Inevitably on these trips, students get in accidents and suffer injuries. It is just part of skiing or snowboarding. Still, there are always parents and families suing the hill, the school, the teachers — anyone — because their kid got lost, skied out of bounds, tried a trick and got hurt. The implication of this kind of lawsuit is that anyone who works with groups of children absolutely has to be covered in every way possible, while insurance companies are increasingly leery of quoting for any group that is not certified, affiliated, recognizable and large-scale.

This logic hits the ground with building and safety inspectors, codebooks in hand. Historically, the greatest impediments to alternative schools have been building codes. A small school can have

"She was one of more than two dozen students ... in Toledo who were arrested in school in October for offenses like being loud and disruptive, cursing at school officials, shouting at classmates and violating dress code. They had all violated the city's safe school ordinance. In cities and suburbs around the country, schools are increasingly sending students into the juvenile justice system for the sort of adolescent misbehaviour that used to be handled by school administrators. In Toledo and many other places the juvenile detention center has become an extension of the principal's office. School officials say they have little choice." *New York Times*, January 4, 2004, p. A1, A15.

7. "High schools across [Canada] are beefing up their security

measures, forcing students to wear visible identification cards and keeping tabs on them with video cameras and security guards. Having to deal with more computer thefts, as well as drug dealing and bullying on school grounds, principals and teachers are not waiting for direction from their school boards on how to curb these problems.... Bruce Cameron, central coordinating principal of school services for the

the students, the parents, the staff, the pedagogical approach, the funds and the equipment in place, but finding a building is often the hardest piece of the puzzle, not because the school has unreasonable expectations for its facility, but because of city codes.

> *The building codes, so blatantly and often tragically ignored in cases of old, collapsing, rat-infested tenement houses owned by landlords who have friends within the city's legal apparatus, are viciously and selectively enforced to try to keep the Free School people out of business....*
>
> *In Boston it is easier to start a whorehouse, a liquor store, a pornography shop or a bookie joint than it is to start a little place to work with children.[12]*

This became clear to me one September some years ago as I stood in front of a building my partner Selena and I had rented for our small community school, staring at a sausage-fingered fire inspector. We had already got the building through the city planning and zoning departments. We had passed our safety, building, fire, earthquake, plumbing, electrical and engineering inspections, and now this guy wanted to do one more fire-safety inspection. It was a couple of weeks into the school year, and our project was teetering on the edge of extinction. We couldn't keep running the school out of parks and beaches anymore; we needed our building.

The guy was glaring at us, ticking off the reasons he would not sign off on this building until we had installed sprinklers throughout, built one more layer of fire protection for all the walls of the 3,300-square-foot facility and added half an inch to each of the twenty-eight stairs. I suggested that we could make those changes incrementally through the year and that we were as interested in the well-being of our students as he was. He said, "No, you are not moving in there until I say it is 100 percent safe for all the kids." I mentioned that the estimates on the work totalled a little more than $35,000, a prohibitive amount. He shrugged.

Still incredulous I asked, "Are you telling me that our four-year-old, twenty-kid little school is going to be closed down because you are insisting on these changes? Do you understand what is happening here? Can we come to some sort of compromise? Is there any way that we can both get what we want?"

Not my problem. Yes. No. Not unless it's what I want.

Standing there dazed and blinking in the sun, I began to understand.

The man's point echoed the baseline operating rationale for so many inspectors in every city everywhere. It is their job to force every building to be as safe as possible, and they understand that in straight-up physical terms. They are simply not going to be the one to sign off on a building in which a tragedy might conceivably occur. And who can blame them: who wants dead children on their résumé? This guy was not going to be the one whose job would be on the line for not sticking strictly to the codebook, and the building we were looking at had too many variables. And that is where safety and life are at odds: in the unpredictabilities, the endless possibilities.[13]

CANONICAL INSULATION

Pedagogically, this is exactly where schools run into trouble. Compulsory state schooling suggests that it can provide what all students need to grow up right, and that the state is the reasonable arbiter of necessary knowledge. As society becomes ever more diverse and complex, however, that position becomes more and more difficult to maintain. The canon comes under continual attack

Toronto District School Board, said schools, especially in big urban centres, must take necessary security measures. 'If you look at society from a general standpoint, we are moving to a more monitored system,' he said." *Globe and Mail*, January 20, 2004, pp. A1, A8.

8. "A five-year-old girl in St. Petersburg, Florida, who began acting silly during a math exercise, was outraged when her teacher confiscated the jelly beans she was using to count. She threw books and boxes, kicked a teacher in the shins, smashed a candy dish, slugged an assistant principal in the stomach and drew on the walls. Police arrested the child, handcuffed her and held for a brief time in the back of a cruiser." "Social Studies," *Globe and Mail*, March 24, 2005, p. A16.

as the range of student needs, demands and expectations becomes increasingly diverse. The result is a rise in complaints and ultimately lawsuits from kids and parents who claim that their school and/or teachers did not do an adequate job in preparing them intellectually, academically or emotionally for university or the workplace. Teachers/administrators become leery of experimentation, innovation and risk and are compelled to stick more and more tightly to the curriculum. They are further constrained by national and international standards, testing and grading. As the range of subjects becomes restricted, monitoring increases, teachers are held accountable for student performance and the possibilities for anomalous experience shrink.

This intensifying fixation on quantitative assessment is making the future of compulsory schooling clearer and clearer. The No Child Left Behind Act, which is driving schools all across the United States to focus on "the basics," punishes, with major fiscal penalties, school boards where test scores are weak. The looming threat to districts that are already stretched to the limit means a continual narrowing of the curriculum, vastly increasing the time spent on reading and math (which are nationally tested) and chopping other classes and activities that are not subject to federal examinations.

The intense focus on the two basic skills is a sea change in American instructional practise, with many schools that once offered rich curriculums now systematically trimming courses like social studies, science and art. A nationwide survey by a nonpartisan group that is to be made public on March 28th [2006] indicates that the practise, known as narrowing the curriculum, has become standard procedure in many communities.

The survey, by the Center on Education Policy, found that since the passage of the federal law, 71 percent of the nation's 15,000 school districts had reduced the hours of instructional time spent on history, music and other subjects to open up more time for reading and math.

"Narrowing the curriculum has clearly become a nationwide pattern," said Jack Jennings, the president of the center....

"Because of its [No Child Left Behind's] emphasis on testing and accountability in particular subjects, it apparently forces some school districts down narrow intellectual paths," Dr. Reese [a University of Wisconsin professor] said. "If a subject is not tested, why teach it?"[14]

Plainly put, kids should spend their days being challenged intellectually, socially and physically. Schools challenge students' patience, their capacity to accept petty authority, their ability to negotiate bureaucracies and their ability to follow orders, which

9. I swear I didn't make that up.

10. "Schools use smart cards to track students," *Vancouver Sun*, December 7, 2005, p. A1, 2.

11. I'm thinking of daycares, community centres, teams, clubs etc.

12. Jonathan Kozol, *Free Schools* (New York: Bantam Books, 1973), pp. 27–28.

13. In the end, our school had to close. Suffice to say, the inspector got his way. It worked out, as we merged our school with another one, but that's a long story. That building and our failure to get it through the

are all good skills to have, but should not be the dominant aspects of a kid's day. Only the very best schools actively attempt to challenge their students' best capacities: it is simply too dangerous. The demands on most schools are so heavy that they understandably choose the safest, least risky choices.

When schools retreat into the same haze of mall, television, video games and movies that so much of childhood has been reduced to today, the possibilities of identity are necessarily reduced.

Manuel Castells describes identity as "the process of construction of meaning on the basis of a cultural attribute, or related set of cultural attributes, that is/are given priority over other sources of meaning." He further distinguishes identity from "roles" like mother, neighbour, smoker, churchgoer, etc., but argues that although identities can be "originated from dominant institutions, they become identities only when and if social actors internalize them, and construct their meaning around this internalization."[15]

Canonical interpretations of education invoke what Castells calls *legitimizing identity*, a universalized ethos that claims what one needs to know can only be authorized by dominant institutions and that without that knowledge you are going to be left on the outside, perennially "left behind." This is a state that "Foucault and Sennett, and before them Horkheimer and Marcuse, see as internalized domination and legitimation of an over-imposed, undifferentiated, normalizing identity."[16]

code was the end of that school as in independent entity.

14. Sam Dillon, "Schools Cut Back Subjects to Push Reading and Math," *New York Times*, March 26, 2006, pp. A1, A18.

15. Manuel Castells, *The Power of Identity* (Oxford: Blackwell, 1997), pp. 6–7.

16. Ibid., p. 9.

Viewed broadly, the whole security apparatus surrounding schools[17] is the functional expression of the belief that educational bureaucracies are capable of defining what people need to know. Once schools start with that premise, and compulsory state schools necessarily do, then the enforcement is self-justifying. Thus "education" becomes a for-your-own-good process of instilling certain canonical knowledge as quickly and as efficiently as possible. It is what Paulo Freire called the "banking method of education."

> Education thus becomes an act of depositing, in which the students are depositories and the teacher is the depositor. . . . in which the scope of action allowed to the students extends only so far as receiving, filing and storing the deposits. They do, it is true, have the opportunity to become collectors or cataloguers of the things they store. But in the last analysis, it is the people themselves who are filed away through the lack of creativity, transformation, and knowledge in this (at best) misguided system. For apart from inquiry, apart from the praxis, individuals cannot be truly human. Knowledge emerges only through invention and reinvention, through the restless, impatient, continuing, hopeful inquiry human beings pursue in the world, with the world and with each other.[18]

The application of what Freire describes came home to me some years ago when I was taking a train from Montreal to Prince Edward Island. I was sharing my compartment with four older women who were returning home after a weekend of gambling in Quebec. They were giddy and fun to be with. In time they found out I was heading to PEI to teach a course called The Philosophy of Education. They were delighted: all were former teachers. As one of them said, to gales of laughter, "I taught seventh grade for almost forty years, honey. And there's only one thing you need to know: sometimes you can't pour a gallon into a cup."

GETTING THE JOB DONE

In this light, it is easy to make sense of the cameras, the security guards, the compulsory attendance, the ID tags, the surveillance, the threats, the coercion. They are extensions of the same school logics that make possible standardized curriculums and their attendant mechanisms of grading and (inter)national standards.[19]

If a comprehensible re-vision of safety is to be imagined, it has to have personal responsibility at its heart: people must learn how to make real choices about their lives from an early age. The vast bulk

17. By this I am referring to the whole constellation of tools, technologies and techniques enforcing school attendance, legitimate behaviour and social relationships.

18. Paulo Freire, "The 'Banking' Concept of Education," in *The Paulo Freire Reader*, Ana Maria Araujo Freire and Donaldo Macedo, eds. (New York: Continuum, 1998), pp. 67–68.

19. There is a huge and growing interest in global standards that measure school performance in various countries against one

of schools offer their students the bare minimum of democratic control or actual decision-making power. To speak of personal choice in school is to speak inside a white noise of discordance.

When local knowledge, local epistemologies and local pedagogies are conflated and displaced by nationalized (and rapidly globalized[20]) curriculums, the possibilities of understanding what it will take for a child to flourish are catastrophically reduced. That is to say, when we expect children to learn the same things at the same rates and in the same sequence,[21] we reduce child rearing, an activity that lies at the heart of human existence, to an industrial activity governed by probability theory.

The factors necessary for children to flourish, however, are inherently enigmatic and depend on such a wide range of factors that standardized testing rarely bears any significant relationship to reality.[22] But to reverse the trend toward global compulsory schooling, we have to root the logic out at its source.

THIS SCHOOL IS THE FUTURE: THAT'S WHY THERE ARE SECURITY CAMERAS EVERYWHERE

another. You've probably seen signs of this in your local paper when you read that Japanese students are ahead of Canadian kids in math, who are behind Scandinavians in science, etc. UNESCO is perhaps the largest force in this project. See for example the UNESCO Institute for Statistics' *Global Education Digest* (www. uis.unesco.org/ e.php?ID=5728_ 201&ID2=DO_ TOPIC). "The UIS [Unesco Institute for Statistics] strives to help countries collect timely data of integrity which meet the dual

There is a little town in the Northwest Territories that I go to called Fort Good Hope. It's approximately 750 kilometres northwest of Yellowknife, almost exactly where the Mackenzie River crosses the Arctic Circle. It is profoundly isolated in many ways, yet entirely within the grasp of popular commodity culture, largely via television. Dominantly Dene, with a Métis minority, the community is experiencing turbulent times. It is emerging from the ashes of residential schools, struggling with colonialism, besieged by drugs and alcohol, attempting to negotiate the relationship between traditions and modernity.

As in so many isolated native communities, there are myriad endemic problems, each intricately tied to all the others. The mix of issues and factors is so complex, so amazingly complicated for a town of 800 people, that I can only glimpse it in my short visits. There are intense layers of bureaucracy, power and control, and potentiality, many of them consistently at odds with one another. The kids in town are in a whirlpool. So many want to leave, but they are tied to family and community so tightly that most who do leave return quickly. Many are bored, some succumb to violence and substance abuse, everyone sees impossible futures on TV every day.

To understand the lives of kids in Good Hope and what they need to thrive is an incredibly complex project. One day, as part of my effort to get to know the place, I visited the school, which physically looms over the town. All kids are expected to attend. My colleague Mark and I found the principal and several teachers, who we were told were rarely seen in town. The principal, a big white guy from Newfoundland, all authority and bluster, gruff ideas and finality, had arrived for his first year at the school just three months earlier.

We asked about his experience so far, and he told us about the numerous arson attempts on the school, the theft problem, the drinking at night and said they were currently installing security cameras all around the perimeter of the facility. We asked why so few kids came to school and why so few of those stayed. He spoke of the terrible state of families in the community, claimed that very few supported the school, and said that most parents didn't want to see their kids get ahead. We asked why there were only southern white teachers at the school. He said no locals were qualified.

Then we talked of the relationship between the school and the larger town. There was a major community gathering that night. For some reason neither the principal nor the teachers had heard of it. In such a small place that seemed strange. The principal went on a bit of a tear. He said that relationships with the chief, the band council and the leadership of the community at large were not great, that no one had invited him, that he was never invited to those kinds of events. He said that people didn't want kids coming to school, didn't want the school to succeed in its mandate because so many adults had "skeletons in their closet." The principal's feeling was that when kids came to school, found counsellors and were willing to talk about their lives, too many problems, too many issues would come out, and that's what the local people were afraid of.

We asked if perhaps after the incursions of the Catholic Church, after the monstrosity of residential schools, in the midst of colonialism, native people might be suspicious of white folks purporting to have answers to their problems. He said he didn't see that at all. His huge fingertip hit the table: *This school is the future of this community.*" End of story.

He articulated clearly (and maybe most honestly) what is at the heart of most schools, just a little more crassly. It is this "for your own good" belief that is so pervasive and bears so much weight when thinking about safety. The core discourses are all about the fundamentalist belief that professionalized institutions simply know what is best for the people they have taken into their care. They are what Ivan Illich has termed *disabling professions*, which actively remove power from individuals and bestow it on those

requirements of relevance to national policies and compliance with international data standards. This will permit regional and global pictures to be drawn and cross-national comparisons to be made." (From the UIS website.)

20. As Article 26 of the 1948 Universal Declaration of Human Rights states, "Elementary education shall be compulsory." UNESCO, in 1951, announced that "the principle of universal compulsory education is no longer questioned."

21. Which is what (to pick just two examples) the No Child Left Behind Act in the United States and Canada's provincial examinations for high school students specifically intend.

22. See Alfie Kohn, *The Case Against Standardized Testing:*

professionalized service providers who are convinced that value is necessarily created only with their intervention.

> Many students, especially those who are poor, intuitively know what the schools do for them. They school them to confuse process and substance. Once these become blurred, a new logic is assumed: the more treatment there is, the better are the results; or, escalation leads to success. The pupil is thereby "schooled" to confuse teaching with learning, grade advancement with education, a diploma with competence, and fluency with the ability to say something new. His imagination is "schooled" to accept service in the place of value.[23]

Much as we try to control nature, we seek to standardize, through schooling, the lives of children with a globalizing logic that reduces self-reliance to a very poor sister to professional service. School people, by identifying a specific and comprehensible Western canon of knowledge and mandating it as necessary, are thereby encumbered with the job of providing that knowledge by almost any means necessary. Schools are then perceived as essential, and child rearing is governed by a series of calculated calculations to determine the least risky choices.

Raising the Scores, Ruining the Schools (Portsmouth, NH: Heinemann, 2000); Peter Sacks, *Standardized Minds: The High Price of America's Testing Culture and What We Can Do to Change It* (Cambridge, MA: Perseus Books, 1999); Deborah Meier, *Many Children Left Behind: How the No Child Left Behind Act Is Damaging Our Children and Our Schools* (Boston: Beacon Press, 2004).

23. Ivan Illich, *Deschooling Society* (New York: Harper & Row, 1970), p. 1.

CRIME PREVENTION NOTICE

DID YOU KNOW? Auto crime hurts a lot of people every year in British Columbia. The costs in claims costs alone total more than $150 million per year. Victims' lost time, property replacement, vehicle rental and insurance deductibles add even more. Add policing and court costs and you can see what a huge problem this is. Prevention is the only way to put a dent in these figures. **You can help.** A police officer or community volunteer noticed your vehicle for the reason stated below.

LOCATION:
☐ PARKING LOT _____
    (NAME)
☐ UNDERGROUND PARKING - ☐ SECURED ☐ OPEN _____
    (NAME)
☑ RESIDENTIAL *1522 Salsbury* _____
    (LOCATION)

DATE: *April 3/04*

☐ **KEYS LEFT IN VEHICLE**

☐ **GARAGE DOOR OPENER LEFT IN VEHICLE**

☐ **VEHICLE LEFT UNLOCKED**

☐ **WINDOW OPEN**

☐ **STEERING WHEEL LOCK**   ☐ in use   ☐ not in use

☐ **VEHICLE EQUIPPED WITH ALARM/IMMOBILIZER**

☐ **POSSESSIONS OR CASH IN VIEW**

☐ **INSURANCE DECAL EXPIRED**

☐ **INSURANCE DECAL BUILDUP**

☑ **ANTI-THEFT DEVICE IN USE. GOOD WORK.**

☑ **YOU'VE TAKEN CARE TO PREVENT AUTO CRIME. THANKS!**

Comments: _____
_____
_____

WARNING For your own protection, please secure your vehicle night and day. Keep your spare key in your wallet, not on the vehicle, and remove all your belongings. Don't leave anything behind. See the other side of this notice for more ways to protect yourself from auto crime.

Grandview
Community Policing Centre
(604) 717-2932

ISSUED BY _____   NUMBER _____

CHAPTER SEVEN

Insert Favourite Lawyer Joke:

The Assignment of Responsibility

Written with much help from Sean Hern

If everyone had done his job, your son would be alive this morning and safely in school. I will simply find out who did not do his job. Then, in your name . . . I will sue that person and the company or agency he works for, I will sue them for negligence. . . .

Was it the fault of the State of New York for not replacing the guardrail out there on the Marlowe road? Was it the fault of the town highway department for having dug a sandpit and let it fill with water? What about the seat belts that had tied so many children into their seats while the rear half of the bus filled with icy water? Was it the governor's fault, then, for having generated legislation that required seat belts? Who caused this accident anyhow? Who can we blame?

RUSSELL BANKS, *The Sweet Hereafter*

The ubiquity of lawsuits is an easy signpost on the path of contemporary absurdity and is one of the first things people point to when they speak of factors undermining anomalous behaviour. The insurance and litigation industries have become intricately bound up with one another, suggesting a social sphere composed of monads, where personal responsibility is displaced by legal and institutionally mediated responsibilities. Everything — every injury, every life, every neurosis — has a price, and every mistake can be costed. The art of the possible has largely been reduced to the art of the insurable.

Like most everyone else, I have spent hours with insurance agents, looking at every kind of coverage under the sun, from liability to third party to accident to board, trying to protect myself, the projects I run and their boards from crippling lawsuits. Most of us implicitly or explicitly cushion our private and professional lives with layer upon layer of coverage, anticipating litigation at every turn, trying to predict the unpredictable and protect ourselves against every circumstance.

My impulse is to describe the lawsuit/insurance worlds as a cabal run by thugs operating patently extortionist schemes, and there might be something there. But it won't get me very far. Political and cultural conversations about blame, responsibility and control continue to lead us down a litigious path, one that appears more absurd at every turn. That said, within tort and insurance discourses there are important ideas about formalized public protection for individuals, and how they are resolved speaks volumes about the nature of our social and political direction.

Insurantial discourses are predicated on three core assumptions. First, that it is possible to evaluate the probability of a given risk. Second, that the risk is collective, not individual. "Strictly speaking there is no such thing as individual risk; otherwise insurance would be no more than a wager."[1] Third, that what is being insured against can be expressed as capital, or priced out. Everything has to be costed. The point is to be able to reduce events to algorithms, create risk categories, collectivize the exposure and add a profit margin.

> *Insurance, therefore, is a means for dealing with the vagaries of fate, a technology through which risk is constructed as a schema of rationality, of ordering elements of reality allowing for a certain way of objectifying things, people and the relationships between them. Insurers "produce risk" by rendering a range of phenomena into a risk — death, bankruptcy, litigation, an accident, a disease, a storm — through specialized actuarial calculations available to them, and then offer guarantees against them. These phenomena would have once been accepted with fatalistic resignation: now they have become objects of risk, given value via the compensation that has been calculated for them. . . . Participation in insurance is about conducting one's life as an enterprise, to ensure that even when misfortune occurs, it is planned for.*[2]

The prevalence of insurantial discourses means everyone has a stake in everyone else not taking chances. Thus everyone, especially those people who manage public spaces, wants you to take fewer risks, be careful, watch out, obey the instructions, stay on the path. Public officials increasingly see public space as littered with lawsuit landmines, and it is the relationship between insurance and liability that makes your behaviour everyone's business.

Insurance, in the form of shared-risk pools, has been documented in many forms from ancient Egypt on, but the origins of the modern insurance industry are usually traced to the late 1500s in London when

1. F. Ewald, quoted in Deborah Lupton, *Risk* (London: Routledge, 1999), p. 95.
2. Ibid., p. 96.

Elizabeth I granted permission to Richard Candaler to establish a Chamber of Insurance to register all insurance transactions in London. By 1688 Edward Lloyd's famous coffee shop on Tower Street was the informal site of a thriving marine insurance centre where merchants, bankers, seafarers and underwriters came together to do business. All these activities meant that businessmen and merchants were free to broaden their scope, even to finance several ships, secure in the knowledge that one tragedy at sea would not wipe them out.[3]

It was marine and merchant interests that kick-started the insurance industry, but it was the Great Fire of London in 1666 that really propelled its development. The year after the fire, several companies began to offer fire insurance.

In those days, insurance premiums were calculated on the assumption that 1 house in 200 would burn down every 15 years. One early fire insurance office in 1680 set its premiums at 2.5% of the annual rent for a brick house and 5% for a wooden one.[4]

Since then the industry has developed exponentially, and the sophistication of its calculations continues to improve both in accuracy and profitability. By 2003, for example, Canadian insurance companies had demonstrably and emphatically rebounded from the chaos into which their industry was thrown after 9/11: "Canada's insurance companies set a record $2 billion profit in 1997 and then watched their profits decrease every year until 2003 when they skyrocketed to $2.63 billion — a 673 per cent increase over the year before.[5]

SUE THE BASTARDS, INSURE THE BASTARDS

Liability cuts both ways, and numerous times I have seen people excited at the prospect of a financial windfall following an accident. I have spoken with kids shortly after they've been hit by a car. They're humming with adrenaline, exaggerating their injuries, hoping for some huge insurance settlement. My family has a good friend who was rear-ended while driving someone else's car. It was a minor accident but certainly the other driver's fault. In the end our friend received a ten-grand settlement. She had some whiplash and a bit of a sore back, but nothing serious, and the ten grand was a small, bizarre miracle to her. She did nothing to overemphasize her wounds; she was uncomfortable for a few weeks, but missed no

3. From a history of insurance presented on the Insurance Bureau of Canada website (www.ibc.ca/gii_history.asp).

4. Ibid.

5. "Insurance profits hit $2.6 billion," *CBC New Brunswick*, March 17, 2004 (www.cbc.ca/nb/story/nb_insuranceprofits20040316.html).

work, and there were no lasting implications. Nevertheless, she was thrilled to get the loot.

6. See purplethistle.ca for more info.

This scenario is repeated every day in every jurisdiction in North America. People jostle and manoeuvre, hoping someone else gets blamed and that maybe they'll find some easy cash. Lawyers push the liability envelope further and further, every enterprise and institution is forced to make adjustments, insurance costs become more and more comprehensive, and public life becomes more expensive, less possible and increasingly standardized.

△

In my case, as director of the Purple Thistle, a youth/community project in East Vancouver,[6] everything I do involves consulting with an insurance agent, real or imagined. *A Food-Not-Bombs free food day in the park?* Lovely idea. I wonder what would happen if someone got food poisoning and sued us? *A camping trip?* Let's do it. What happens if someone gets lost, the van crashes, someone breaks an ankle hiking? *Going out the back door?* Be careful that you don't fall down. These kinds of discourses are my everyday reality.

My personal impulse at my workplace, as it probably is for many other people, is to say *Screw it. If it seems like a good, fun, interesting idea, it's worth doing. If something happens, we'll deal with it then.*

But the questions can never be only are we taking due and appropriate precautions or is the activity a good and useful one. Those are factors, but the bottom line is whether or not it will be covered by our insurance. That seems crazy, but it's true. Very often I ignore grey areas, take risks, organize or agree to projects that may or may not fit within our coverage, but that just isn't a good idea.

If something were to happen for which our centre wasn't covered — like, say, a kid playing hockey in the back alley was hit by a car (we have on-site coverage, but off-site only for specific events) — there might be real trouble. My initial response is *Go ahead, sue my ass. I'm broke and you're getting nothing.* But as my insurance broker has patiently explained to me many times, if our non-profit society were to be sued, the lawyers would go after the organization. And since the organization has few appreciable assets, they could then go after the board of directors and their personal assets.

That means that members of the board, composed largely of my dear friends, could possibly have their houses expropriated should any major lawsuit be brought against our organization. A youth non-profit society to which they generously donate their time and energy could potentially cost them their beloved and hard-

earned homes due to some perceived supervisory lapse on my part. Believe me, I think about this every time a kid comes and proposes a project, any project, whether it's feeding homeless people or building a porch or going on a trip. Could this be costing my friends their houses? Sure, that's paranoid and unhealthy and unlikely, but it is reality and it governs my decision making in so many ways, on so many fronts.

7. "Snowboard accident brings suit," *Vancouver Sun*, April 26, 2000, p. B4.

8. "Alberta to allow unborn injured in car crash to sue mother," *Vancouver Sun*, November 3, 2005, p. A4.

9. Reuters Wire report, March 7, 2005.

△

There is no need to catalogue the litany of bizarre and/or incomprehensible lawsuits that have been filed and won significant damages. You read about them constantly: the guy who sued the roller rink for not telling him that roller blading was potentially dangerous; bars that have been sued by drunks for letting them drink too much; schools sued when kids leave not smart enough. How about this one: A kid was paralyzed at a local ski hill and the parents sued the hill, the school and everyone involved, claiming in part that the hill was negligent for depicting "jumping with a snowboard as an exciting and adventurous activity when it knew or ought to have known that the activity had great potential danger."[7]

Or the recent decision of the Alberta government to introduce legislation allowing children to sue their mothers for injuries suffered while still in the womb, mimicking existing laws in the United Kingdom.[8] Or the lawsuit filed in New York in March 2005 on behalf of tsunami victims, mainly European plaintiffs, claiming that Thai and US forecasters failed to give adequate warning of the wave's approach. The suit also named the French Accor group, owner of a hotel chain, as negligent for failing to equip its spa and resort "with state-of-the-art seismic detection and warning systems, despite its location 'in an earthquake and tsunami fault zone.'"[9]

Amidst all the foolishness, there is something important going on. Perhaps this tsunami of lawsuits and insurance claims is nothing more than whacked lawyers realizing they can get rich quick chasing ambulances. Perhaps everyday people are just piling on the bandwagon, adopting litigious logic in an attempt to turn some easy cash. Maybe it is a function of an insanely consumerist culture that wants to get rich or die trying. Maybe it is an ugly phenomenon that will abate once legal loopholes are closed and litigation fatigue sets in. I doubt it, though.

WATCH YOURSELF

ALL TORTED UP

To understand the development of litigiousness, it is important
to understand the basics of tort law. A "tort" is a wrongful act that
someone commits against someone else. The distinction between a
tort and a criminal act is that the state prosecutes the latter on society's behalf, whereas the prosecution of the former is a matter of
private law between the person who claims to have suffered injury
and those who are alleged to have caused it.

There are two categories of tort law: intentional torts and negligence. Intentional torts are wilful acts committed by one person
against another (or against another's property) and include battery
and assault, conversion (theft), fraud, defamation and the like.
Negligence, on the other hand, describes a wrong done to another
person accidentally. There is no intent to injure the other person.
Instead, one person was careless and her careless acts injured
someone she ought to have known would be hurt if proper care
were not taken. Negligence is the typical personal injury action for
car accidents, slips and falls, etc.

Negligence has three fundamental components. First, there must
exist a duty of care from one person to the other. Each of us has a
duty at law to conduct ourselves in a manner that does not place
those around us in harm's way. Thus a shopkeeper has a duty of
care to his customers. A homeowner has a duty of care to her neighbours and guests. A driver of a car has a duty of care to the other
drivers on the road. And so on.

The second component of negligence is that the appropriate
standard of care must be breached by the person who has a duty of
care. So the shopkeeper does not have a responsibility to protect his
customers from every possible risk. That standard of care would be
too high. However, if the shopkeeper mopped the tiles of his shop
and did not bother to warn anyone that they would be unusually
slippery, he would likely have breached the standard of care he
owed to his customers.

The third component of a negligence claim is that the aggrieved
party must suffer injuries or damages. There is no negligence, for
example, when the shopkeeper mops down the tiles but no one is
injured. "I might have been killed" does not constitute negligence
(unless the mere presence of the threat caused psychological
distress).

There are tens of thousands of cases that refine these principles in
the context of different negligence scenarios, but the basics remain

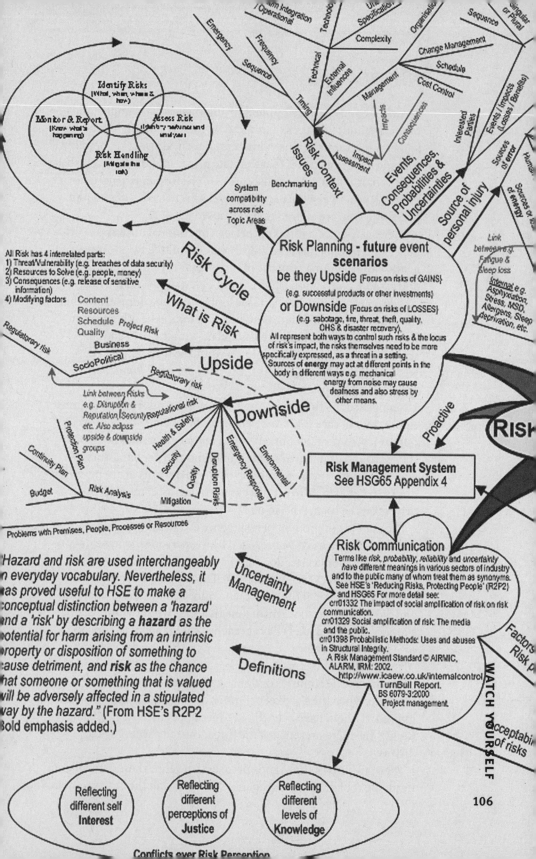

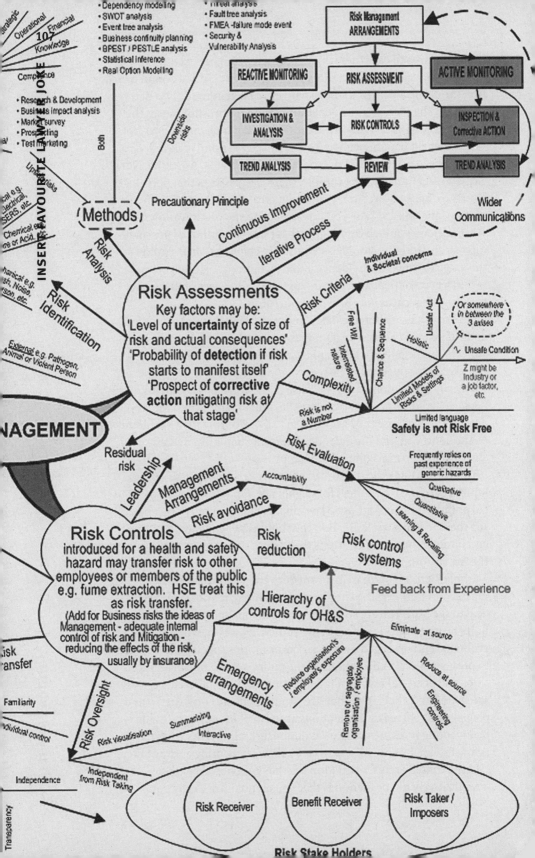

the same. In each case there is a constant tension between what kind of risk is acceptable in our society and what kind of compensation should be awarded to those who have been injured. This determination changes over the generations, and in threshold cases the judges decide which risks are acceptable and which aren't.

Another element of negligence law to keep in mind is the effect of negligence legislation. In England, the United States, Australia, New Zealand and Canada, for example, there is legislation that permits courts to "apportion" damages, which creates a defence of "contributory negligence." If I sue you, the negligence legislation allows you to defend yourself by alleging that I was the author of my own misfortune and therefore "contributorily negligent." It also allows the judge to weigh the evidence and levy out proportional blame — i.e., 5 percent here and 50 percent there. The effect of this is that even hopeless cases may be worth pursuing.

Let's say I have suffered catastrophic injuries because I was drunk and walked into a bus. The fault is almost entirely mine, but it is still worth suing the bus driver for negligence because if I can find something to suggest that he was even 2 percent liable, it may be worth my while monetarily. Because of the concept of contributory negligence, some people speculate that judges have raised the standard of care because they know it isn't all or nothing for a defendant — the court can find the defendant partially liable but make a soft award and keep everyone sort of happy.

There are some other factors to consider in the propensity of injured people to sue others for negligence. First, the growth of corporations has encouraged lawsuits. People generally don't like to sue their neighbours. Suing Bob the shopkeeper can have emotional and interpersonal ramifications that do not exist where one is suing the Acme Company.

Similarly, the growth in insurance coverage has tremendous ramifications. If Bob the shopkeeper is insured, it's not such a big deal to sue him. You are suing Bob in form, but you are really suing Bob's insurer. No one's life is being ruined. However, when risks are evaluated and managed by private corporations specifically devoted to profit, cultural expectations of the public sphere, social relationships and personal responsibility become radically altered; as risks are shared and alleviated, they are simultaneously constructed and propagated. There is a tremendous amount of money to be made by inventing risks, warning us assiduously and then insuring us against them. It is a business strategy that is becoming a way of life.

In the United States, a situation that has contributed to the lawsuit-happy phenomenon is that you do not have to pay your

Life's an investment with great returns.

109

TD Waterhouse offers a full range of services to help you achieve your goals.

You can work because you need to, or you can work because you want to. You can provide an education for your children, or you can provide the education your children deserve. You can pass it on or you can leave a legacy. At TD Waterhouse, we will tell you what you can expect from us and how we will help you achieve your financial goals. We are devoted to helping you, so you can make the most of life. Call us today.

DISCOUNT BROKERAGE | FINANCIAL PLANNING | PRIVATE CLIENT SERVICES

1 866 280-2022

opponent's costs if you lose a lawsuit. (In Canada, on the other hand, if you go to trial and lose, you can face a bill for legal costs in the tens of thousands of dollars. That is a significant disincentive to pursue a case to trial.) In the United States, the ramifications of no costs and a contingency fee set-up, in which the lawyer generally foots the bill for the action and takes a percentage of the award only if she wins, are that there is endless incentive for an injured person to sue — all benefit, no burden. This is why the United States, as well as most industrialized countries, is trying to develop legislation to curtail the growth in personal injury litigation.

One of the more beneficial aspects of tort law is that it has been used to hold corporate polluters, drug companies and cigarette manufacturers somewhat responsible for their actions and to hold them fiscally accountable to a degree. Exxon, cigarette and auto companies, for example, have all paid richly and very publicly for some of their negligences.

Torts have emerged as one occasionally viable way for communities to defend themselves against corporate crime, even as trade agreement proponents try to dismantle the little legal protection that exists. This is why talk about tort reform is all the rage in American conservative circles, where the conversation is often about limiting the damage individuals and communities can do to corporate freedom. "Tort reform" as a continuing issue is largely about removing the barriers to corporate movement and reducing their degree of liability exposure.

△

It is important to remember that there are legitimate and justifiable rationales behind tort laws. The principles are important when people suffer catastrophic injuries from other people's negligence. If a child is put in a coma for a year and rendered a quadriplegic for the rest of her life after being hit by a drunk driver, somebody should pay so the family is not destroyed. The insurance system provides that she will see some real dollars rather than whatever was in the drunk's bank account.

The logic of insurance partially relies on a pastoral resonance: the idea of a community chest, of socially shared responsibility, of the collective assumption of risk. These are critical values, but as is so familiar in hyper-capitalism, this vision has been distorted, often beyond recognition. It is important that social structures exist to share risk and to prevent individuals who have suffered harm being left to deal with the consequences on their own. There is a fundamental difference, however, between people knowing the risks they are taking and corporate greed deliberately creating and/or obscuring risks to the public. When profit is the benchmark, risk becomes very political.

For example, deliberately hiding the actual contents of cigarettes and ignoring the profound health risks of smoking is patently wrong. Perpetrating environmental destruction and toxification and refusing to adequately clean up is wrong. On the other hand, not explicitly and repeatedly reminding snowboarders that the activity is dangerous strikes me as just fine. This leaves us again with what is reasonable. The critical issues in insurance appear to rest on three complementary values: the cultural importance of self-reliance; the value of shared risk at the community level; the inadequacy of profit-centric organizations to drive safety and risk discourses.

Given these values as a baseline, and I suggest that they are commonly held, we need to reconstruct institutions that buffer individuals against catastrophic damage and establish community-based structures that share risk and liability beyond the privately controlled, greed-driven companies that are so distorting public relationships.

I believe it is possible to imagine municipalized institutions that provide the best of what insurance companies now purport to cover while mitigating their predatory behaviour. In a world where money buys justice, it is hardly reasonable to expect the legal system to correct itself. We need genuine tort reform that is about protecting individuals and communities and restricting the scope of corporate power. Then we can reconsider safety in a community context and re-establish the kinds of local institutions and relation-ships that once shared the assumption of risk beyond the call of greed.

FIND YOUR INNER LEWIS & CLARK.

WATCH YOURSELF

112

CHAPTER EIGHT

All Those People Out There:

Technology and the Reinvention

of Public Life

The magic of electronic communications makes direct democracy inevitable. Does this signal the dissolution of government as we know it? Unquestionably.

FRANK OGDEN, *Navigating in Cyberspace*

When television has fulfilled its ultimate destiny, man's sense of physical limitation will be swept away . . .

DAVID SARNOFF, QUOTED IN *Tube: The Invention of Television*

You are my creator, but I am your master.

FRANKENSTEIN'S MONSTER IN MARY SHELLEY'S *Frankenstein*

1. "Fossil's SPOT wristwatch will provide access to about a dozen personalized channels of information, such as sports, weather, news, and to-do lists, and will be able to receive text messages, Fossil's [Donald] Brewer says. Wearers will navigate the watch's LCD display using only buttons.

"Brewer expects the first Fossil watches to ship late this year at prices between $100 and $250, with a monthly data subscription fee of about $10. The watches must be recharged

Most of us have a reflexive fascination for new technologies and gadgets, often for good reason. After the initial amazement at an iPod or wireless mouse or whatever, people tend to consider how the gadget might be useful in their lives and whether they can afford it. There is a nearly universal attraction that ranges from mild curiosity to reverence. Personally, I'm still feeling kind of reverent about Bill Gates's January 2003 unveiling of plans for wristwatches that come with real-time sports score tickers.[1] Simultaneously, though, we tend to have a fear of technology, extravagantly voiced in so many science fiction movies and comic books: a monster is unleashed, a computer starts thinking for itself, robots turn on people.

One of the central aspects of postmodern technologies is their capacity to force a reimagining of what constitutes "the public." Information and communication innovations have focused on squeezing time and space, making it possible for us to contact anyone at any time from any place. It doesn't matter what city or what time; the question is always, Where do you want to go today? The assumption is that we escape our bonds, and no part of the world, no person, is inaccessible. The idea of the public that we are part of has been expanded to include everywhere: the global village.

This expansion is also a function of hyper-capitalism and globalization. "The public" has typically been defined as a large grouping that shares some kind of common interest, something larger than community but smaller than "everyone in the world." However, if we now live in a one-world, flattened place, it can be assumed we all share the same interests: the same buying patterns, the same cultural aspirations, the same desire for a good deal, the same ability to talk to anybody, the same specials. The more ubiquitous communication and information technology becomes, the more Brussels looks like Houston looks like Quito looks like Bangkok looks like Cairo.

Global bond traders, business people and jet-setters love the new possibilities. Franchise opportunities are endless. There are virgin markets everywhere you turn. But the incredible profit potential cannot hide a widespread creeping suspicion, a fear that these "global village" fantasies have become just that, that too many places look too much the same. The same fast-food outlets dominate every big city everywhere. People wear the same Adidas, listen to the same Eminem, carry the same Vuitton knockoffs, dream the same dreams.

Thinking about safety has to include thinking about technology specifically, but also in general: technology is how we defend ourselves from the natural world, disease and toil. It is the mechanism though which we articulate our dreams of predictability.

Is it possible, however, that technology is getting away from us, that it is starting to ride us? Does technology really keep us safe?

BEWARE; FOR I AM FEARLESS

The idea of technology "out of control" is best articulated by Frankenstein's monster: "Beware; for I am fearless and therefore powerful."[2] As Martin Heidegger put it, "technological advance will move faster and faster and can never be stopped. In all areas of his existence, man will be encircled ever more tightly by the forces of technology.[3] From Kant to Ellul[4] to today, the vision of tools with their own will is a titillating one.[5]

Maybe the most forceful repudiation of the idea that the trajectory of technology is beyond human control, however, was laid out by Langdon Winner in *Autonomous Technology*. Winner outlines and historicizes the out-of-control renditions of our technological

every two to three days, and the information is available with a quick peek.

"'This is what we call "glance-ability,"' said Roger Gulrajani, director of marketing for Microsoft's SPOT initiative." Tom Spring, "Next: News, Sports, and Weather on Your Wristwatch," *PCWorld*.com, January 8, 2003. Frankly, I want one of these Fossil watches. Badly. I'm all about "glanceability." Unfortunately the watches didn't do so well due to lousy batteries and dubious convenience and are now available on eBay for about $40, but I don't care. I want one.

2. Mary Shelley, *Frankenstein*, original 1818 text, D.L. Macdonald and K. Scherf, eds. (Peterborough, ON: Broadview, 1994), pp. 194–95.

3. Martin Heidegger, from *Discourse on Thinking*, cited in Langdon Winner, *Autonomous Technology*

relationships, highlighting the power that autonomous technologies supposedly strip from humans: the capacity to control, affect, change or dismantle that which we have built. If our tools have taken on autonomous lives of their own, then analytical and political practices are rendered impotent, leaving us to

> *stand idly by while vast technical systems reverse the reasonable relationship between means and ends. It is here above all that modern men come to accept an overwhelmingly passive response to everything technological. The maxim "What man has made he can also change" becomes increasingly scandalous.*[6]

Winner, echoed by Seymour Melman, Lewis Mumford, Murray Bookchin[7] and many others, calls for humans to regain control of their tools and to rationally reorganize their dispersal and use. He insists

> *that we return to the original understanding of technology as a means that, like all other means available to us, must only be employed with a fully informed sense of what is appropriate. Here, the ancients knew, was the meeting point at which ethics, politics and technics came together. . . .*
> *A sign of the maturity of modern civilization would be its recollection of that lost sense of appropriateness in the judgement of means. . . . There are now many cases in which we would want to say: "After all a temptation is not very tempting."*[8]

But arguing that our tools are controllable should not obscure the tendencies contained within certain tools, nor should it suggest in any way their neutrality. To speak of technology as neutral is a dated project at best,[9] and the idea that tools are simply pieces of metal or wood or plastic is only true at a most basic level. Their creation, deployment, spread and teleology are deeply interrelated with the social and cultural conditions that both produce and maintain them.[10] Tools also carry with them specific tendencies regarding their use and functions. Even in a genuinely democratic and ecological society, for example, a nuclear reactor would maintain its scale, inherent danger and anti-ecological capacities. A broom, on the other hand, can be pretty much understood as a benign tool wherever you are.

In "Women and the Assessment of Technology," Corlann Gee Bush writes that

> *Tools and technologies have what I can only describe as valence, a bias or*

(Cambridge, MA: MIT Press, 1977), p. 14.

4. See especially Jacques Ellul's influential *The Technological Society* (New York: Vintage, 1964). While often misquoted, it retains real import, both because of and despite his insistence on autonomous technologies: "Technique is autonomous with respect to economics and politics . . . technique elicits and conditions social, political, and economic change" (p. 133).

5. Or as Daniel Bell nicely puts it, "in the evolution of technocratic thinking, things began to ride men." "Post-Industrial Society and the Future," in *Man-Made Futures*, Nigel Cross, David Elliott and Robin Roy, eds. (London: Hutchinson Edu-

"charge" analogous to atoms that have lost or gained electrons through ionization. A particular technological system, even an individual tool, has a tendency to interact in similar situations in identifiable and predictable ways.... Valence tends to seek out or fit in with certain social norms and to ignore or disturb others.[11]

It is evident, in the maw of twenty-first-century hyper-capitalism, that many of our tools and our relationships with them illuminate our social relationships. If technology is necessarily positioned in antagonism to nature and reflects the kinds of control we are seeking, what can we infer from new tools?

THINGS RIDE PEOPLE

Many people tend to be suspicious of technology, and the more complex the tool, the more wary folks tend to be. For example, they wonder about the prudence of letting kids play video games for hours every day. Many more are seriously concerned about human genome mapping, genetically engineered foods, cloning and toxic waste. Ulrich Beck has articulated a version of this with his "Risk Society" analysis, arguing that industrial society has moved well past scarcity and production issues, and the minimizing of global risks is now our primary social challenge. In a series of books, Beck develops the idea that modern technology has globalized mass risks (like nuclear power, pollution and global warming) and that risks are now comprehensive.[12]

Riding herd on most of these suspicions is the recurring idea that technology is not keeping us safe; maybe we are keeping *it* safe, at our own peril. Maybe technology is becoming tired of us running the show and is prepared to fight back.

The rhythm of revenge is usually more complex than that, but the question is valid. Consider the case of the SUV. The sport-utility vehicle exploded onto the auto market in the mid-90s to the complete surprise of its manufacturers, who largely considered it a cheap niche-vehicle gimmick that allowed them to avoid safety and emissions regulations by classifying it as a truck rather than a car. The SUV swiftly became an all-time boom story, with Big Three profits riding a wave in large part driven by mythology that SUVs are safer than cars.

The reality, however, is that "SUVs are no safer than cars for their occupants, and pose much greater dangers for other road users.... The occupant death rate in crashes per million SUVs on the road is

cational, 1974), p. 104.

6. Winner, *Autonomous Technology*, p. 314.

7. See Seymour Melman, "The Myth of Autonomous Technology," in *Man-Made Futures*, Nigel Cross, David Elliott and Robin Roy, eds. (London: Hutchinson Educational, 1974); Lewis Mumford, *Technics and Civilization* (New York: Harcourt, Brace and World, 1963) or *The Myth of the Machine* (New York: Harcourt, 1967); or, for example, Murray Bookchin's *Ecology of Freedom* (Palo Alto, CA: Cheshire, 1982), *Urbanization Without Cities* (Montreal: Black Rose, 1992), *Post-Scarcity Anarchism* (Berkeley: Ramparts, 1971), or *The Modern Crisis* (Montreal: Black Rose, 1987).

8. Winner, *Autonomous Technology*, p. 327.

9. Although that hasn't prevented a whole generation of Marxists,

WATCH YOURSELF

116

6 percent higher than the death rate per million cars."[13] As Malcolm Gladwell puts it,

> *minivans, with their unit-body construction, do much better in accidents than SUVs. (In a thirty-five-mph crash test for instance, the driver of a Cadillac Escalade — the GM counterpart to the Lincoln Navigator — has a sixteen-per-cent chance of a life-threatening head injury, a twenty-per-cent chance of a life-threatening chest injury and thirty-five percent chance of a leg injury. The same numbers in a Ford Windstar minivan — a vehicle engineered from the ground up, as opposed to simply being bolted onto a pickup-truck frame — are, respectively, two percent, four percent, and one percent.) But this desire for safety wasn't a rational calculation. It was a feeling.*[14]

The SUV has capitalized relentlessly on a number of car-buying impulses that do not rationally add up, but contribute heavily toward drivers' feeling of safety. Chief among them is height. The ability to look down, to feel bigger and taller, makes SUV owners feel secure, even though they (must) know that the higher you are, the more chance there is of a rollover. Same thing with visibility.

neo-Marxists and critical theorists from bashing their heads against the neutrality wall. Perhaps the best and most layered theorist of this bent is Andrew Feenberg. In *Critical Theory of Technology* (New York: Oxford

Drivers feel more secure with smaller windows that make it harder for others to see inside their vehicle, even if this dangerously cuts down on their own sightlines. "But that's the puzzle of what has happened to the automotive world," writes Gladwell. "Feeling safe has become more important than actually being safe.[15]

Equally important is the menace that SUVs pose to the rest of the world (and that's totally ignoring the larger-scale environmental dangers). SUVs rely on passive safety rather than active safety. Simply put, people believe that because SUVs are bigger, heavier and higher, they will do better if another vehicle crashes into them. Smaller car owners sense their own vulnerability, actively use their better manoeuvrability and are always aware of defensive driving. SUV drivers, convinced of their own invulnerability, move like bullies.

Jettas are safe because they make their drivers feel unsafe. SUVs are unsafe because they make their drivers feel safe. That feeling of safety isn't the solution; it's the problem. . . . In the age of the SUV this is what people worry about when they worry about safety — not risks, however commonplace, involving their own behaviour but risks, however rare, involving some unexpected event.[16]

An October 2005 report in the *British Medical Journal* stated that SUVs are especially dangerous to pedestrians, more than twice as likely as a car to injure or kill a person. Because SUVs are so much higher, pedestrians take the primary impact on their torsos and heads. Smaller vehicles tend to collide primarily with people's legs; their upper bodies take the secondary impact. Researchers are calling for consumers to be warned of these risks before purchase.[17]

However irrational SUV-lust is, the vehicles' popularity forces other drivers' hands. With huge vehicles all over the roads, their bumpers riding a full foot above yours, the urge to get bigger is a powerful one. It was with this in mind that I downloaded information from Homeland Defense Vehicles.[18] My neighbours have an SUV. I've decided to keep up, maybe with a little mustard, and have pretty much settled on the Bad Boy Heavy Muscle Truck (HMT). It's a civilian version of the light tactical military truck used by the US Army: three and a half tons, ten feet tall, with a base price of $225,000.

The price goes up from there, depending on options. Drivers can get infrared cameras that peer through darkness. The flat-nosed cab can be bulletproof, and house a mini-safe behind three leather seats. The dash

University Press, 1991) he writes: "The degradation of labor, education, and the environment is rooted not in technology per se but in the antidemocratic values that govern technological development" (p. 3). Feenberg does attempt a synthesis of what he calls "instrumental and substantive theories" and largely concludes that "the contingency of the existing technological system" can be identified and "invested with new values and bent to new purposes" (p. 196). It is obvious and fundamental to say that tools emerge from the culture and conditions which produced them, but to assume that technologies themselves have little or no dialectical relationship with society is obscurantist.

can include a satellite phone, a two-way radio and a global-positioning system — all alongside DVD, MP3 and CD players and a flip-out LCD screen. For $750,000, buyers can get the fully loaded "NBC" version that can . . . detect and block out fallout from nuclear, biological and chemical weapons by over-pressurizing the cab with filtered, clean air much like an aircraft.[19]

The Bad Boy HMT is real. And don't underestimate its potential. The manufacturer expects sales to start at fifty this year and climb. Riding in the wake of the SUV and the Hummer, who knows?

SO GOOD, SO PERFECT, SO NECESSARY

Sometimes it is hard to grasp the intensity of emotion with which Western culture attaches itself to apparently (or patently) trivial tools. For a cocktail of reasons, gadgets and novelty seize the popular imagination. While salesmanship and marketing hyperbole have much to answer for, there is something else going on too. Consider a July 12, 2000, advertising feature in the *Globe and Mail*, tied in with the introduction in Canada of the Palm Pilot.[20]

> *"The Palm is wearable, elegant and small," he [Michael Moskowitz, president and GM of Palm Canada says, though he admits that those attributes are just the beginning of the explanation. "The Zen of Palm resides in its simplicity, wearability and its style of execution." . . .*
> *It becomes an indispensable part of a person's life. . . . So you can live your life more efficiently. Elegantly. Simply.*[21]

It's perilous to equate over-the-top advertising gibberish with real meaning, but in this case it illustrates a point. It is hard to imagine that anyone could write or read that Palm ad without a certain sense of embarrassment. Palm products are electronic datebooks with Internet access. Their uses are, by definition, trivial. The company backed its claim that the Palm Pilot is indispensable by listing some if its uses, including playing blackjack, keeping golf scores or a workout log, acting as an alarm clock, displaying the periodic table, storing football schedules, playing chess, keeping a diet log, scanning business cards and dozens of similar functions.

There is something untrivial about the way Palms and their kin are bought, sold and used, however, not just because of their artefactual/symbolic value, but because they represented another level of novelty. The reification of novelty in our culture, the fascination

Some tools and technological practices have inherently anti-democratic tendencies in and of themselves. Not all are entirely contingent on external conditions.

10. See, for example, Albert Borgmann's discussion in *Technology and the Character of Contemporary Life* (Chicago: University of Chicago Press, 1984) of "the question of the leeway people have in working out their technological existence . . . People do have choices here" (pp. 103-4).

11. Corlann Gee Bush, "Women and the Assessment of Technology," in *Machina Ex Dea: Feminist Perspectives on Technology*, J. Rothschild, ed. (New York: Pergamon, 1983), p. 155.

12. See *Risk Society* (London: Sage Publications, 1992), *World Risk Society* (Malden,

WATCH YOURSELF

with small-scale fascination, is a backwater flow of what David Nye calls the sublime:

> [It is] not a social residue, created by economic and political forces, though both can inflect its meaning. Rather it is essentially a religious feeling, aroused by the confrontation with impressive objects, such as Niagara Falls, the Grand Canyon, the New York Skyline, the Golden Gate Bridge, or the earth-shaking launch of a space shuttle. The technological sublime is an integral part of contemporary consciousness, and its emergence and exfoliation into several distinct forms during the past two centuries is inscribed within public life.[22]

The reverential qualities assumed to be universally felt by people viewing a crashing waterfall or towering peak are easily inscribed on technologies as well. Spectacularist engineering feats like bridges, dams and skyscrapers are imbued with the same sublime characteristics. It's an easy leap to make when our age has apparently triumphed so convincingly over nature.[23]

If technology is where nature is not, great acts of building are understood as beyond nature in a quasi-spiritual sense. As Nye writes, "In a physical world that is increasingly desacralized, the sublime represents a way to reinvest the landscape and the works of men with transcendent significance."[24] In an age of natural conquest, the challenge, nay obsession, of technological man is to transcend time and space, just as the forest, the sea and the air have been transcended.[25]

Acres of gadgets, innovations and tools have been dumped into Western culture. Right now, approximately 75 new products are introduced to the market every day, for a running total of something like two million.[26] The success or failure of any given product has something to do with its inherent usefulness and value, and plenty to do with the quality of its marketing. It is impossible to think of technology without considering how it is sold, and while some things are explicitly described as pure trivialities, the heart of technological marketing is always about appealing to higher moral ground. Often that means your safety or your family's security.

The idea that technology will keep us safe, insulated from the vagaries and capriciousness of the world, is one that has exploded in the last hundred and fifty years. At one time, personal skill, resourcefulness, courage and sometimes community were regarded as the best (and often only) bulwarks against danger, but increasingly this part of the world relies heavily on technologies, from alarm systems to garage door openers to genetically engineered

MA: Polity Press, 1999) and/or *Ecological Politics in the Age of Risk* (Cambridge: Polity Press, 1995), among others.

13. Keith Bradsher, *High and Mighty: SUVs — the World's Most Dangerous Vehicles and How They Got That Way* (New York: Public Affairs, 2002), p. 427.

14. Malcolm Gladwell, "Big and Bad: How the SUV Ran over Automotive Safety," *New Yorker*, January 12, 2004, p. 28.

15. Ibid., p. 30.

16. Ibid., p. 33.

17. Paul Taylor, "SUVs are hazardous to pedestrian health, researchers warn," *Globe and Mail*, October 7, 2005, p. A13.

18. Check out www.homelanddefensevehicles.com.

19. Kristen Hays,

food to stem cell research, to protect ourselves.

To sell well and persevere, new tools are located within larger rubrics — as necessary pieces of the good life, as transformative and/or liberating. It is critical for technologies to attach themselves to universally attractive virtues, and the most successful marketing campaigns are able to connect the product inextricably to grand ideals.

In the 1990s, for example, the telephone company here in British Columbia, under a deregulatory siege from Shaw, Sprint and all the rest, was aggressively marketing services and a bevy of mobile phones, pagers and other communication technologies with a "*B connected. B free. BCTel*" tag line. Some of the ads had an Archie-comics kind of thrust, warning that the big party was happening and everybody was going to be there except you because you didn't get the call.

Most of the campaign aimed for bigger ground; TV ads showed futuristic scenes of people flitting about on space-age air vehicles, taking calls on their wristwatches, or billboards of underwater panoramas with fish drifting about weightlessly and "Be Free" scripted across the bottom. The message was impossible to miss: Buy this and your life will become weightless, you will come and go as you please. The bonds of your life will fall away in the face of your cell phone.

North Americans are numbed to the built-in ludicrousness of this kind of advertising, but it is effective because it so smoothly blurs the lines between the reality of the product and the vision that is being sold. No one, not even Telus advertising lizards, will claim that a cell phone will make you "free" in the deeper senses of the word.

Taking the dubious convenience of being reachable at any time, naming it "freedom" and then attaching it to compelling visions of larger freedom is the stock-in-trade of marketing hacks. Soon enough, in the face of relentless exposure to this kind of logic, owning only a landline will make your life seem hopelessly constricted and burdened.

Many cell-phone owners beg off in the name of safety, claiming they own their phone for use "in emergencies only." They want a cell just in case they are late to pick up the kids, they find themselves in a dangerous situation, or the mythical flat tire strikes. Except everyone I know never limits themselves to those occasions. They use the cell constantly because it is in their pocket. One consequence is that cell users are on the phone all the time, are constantly checking the thing or text messaging, and are always reachable, a

"New Bad Boy Truck Dwarfs the Hummer," AP Wire report, February 13, 2005.

20. Which is dated already because Palm has been pretty much swamped by BlackBerries and Sidekicks, game-playing TVs, and camera-equipped cell phones.

21. Special Advertising Feature, *Globe and Mail*, July 12, 2000, p. P1.

22. David Nye, *The American Technological Sublime* (Cambridge, MA: MIT Press, 1994), p. xiii.

23. I also want to point out here that human domination of nature is made possible, explicitly, by hierarchy — that is, by human domination of human. "C.S. Lewis once remarked that 'Man's power over Nature often turns out to be a power exerted by some men over other men with Nature as its instrument." Arnold Pacey, *The*

condition that constitutes part of my own private vision of hell.

There's more. Maybe cell phones are not all that healthy to be holding up to your head all day long. There is the socio-psychological annoyance of people never really being where they are, never really being in the place and moment because they are always connected, always thinking about the next call. There is the workaholic lifestyle that is engendered by always being available to talk business, at home, while hiking, on the bus, wherever. I cannot imagine that we would be worse off if all cell phones ceased to exist, and I'm doing what I can here, but I am losing the battle.

Whether it is beer that will make you more rugged, dishwashers that will enable you to spend more time with your kids, or lawn mowers that will make your yard more beautiful, technology has consistently sold itself with evocations of a better world. Technology doesn't just slip seamlessly into the culture; it *becomes* the culture, displacing what was once there. We buffer ourselves with technology, but examples, historical and personal, of "unintended consequences" are too numerous and visceral to ignore. As Neil Postman wrote, "Tools are not integrated into the culture; they attack the culture. They bid to become the culture."[27] After some time, the products or tools and the virtues they profess to inculcate become indistinguishable from one another, at which point your safety is synonymous with your garage-door opener and your phone.

Culture of Technology (Oxford: Basil Blackwell, 1983), p. 12.

24. Nye, *American Technological Sublime*, p. xiii.

25. A number of writers have taken modernity's reverential feeling for machines and named

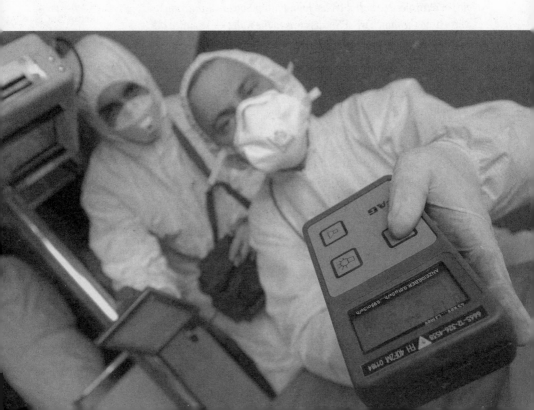

CHADS DANGLE EVERYWHERE: LIBERATING TECHNOLOGY

Most of the lightning-fast changes that are speeding our culture along are being driven by information and communications technology. Almost faster than most of us can keep up, new frontiers of virtuality create evolving conceptions of the idea of "public," with unfamiliar renditions of social relationships en route. Global communications, 24/7 connectivity, wireless technologies and the magic of consumerist ingenuity have rendered many traditional conceptions of "the public" quaint and dated. But if, as Takis Fotopoulos writes, "a democratic science and technology presupposes an inclusive democracy,"[28] the reverse is true as well.

The sheer pace and volume of technological innovation often make it difficult to comprehend the side effects and/or the deeper, longer-term implications of new tools. The introduction of new technologies is met sometimes with unbridled consumer enthusiasm, sometimes with suspicion, and often with a fatalistic shrug of inevitability. It can be difficult to guess what ramifications some tools might have, and the interpretations of those reverberations are equally contentious.

It is notable that even plausible predictions of new inventions can turn out, in retrospect, to be ludicrous. John Phillip Souza — the composer who was to the march what Strauss was to the waltz — regarded the introduction of the phonograph with great foreboding: "I foresee a marked deterioration in American music and musical taste, an interruption in the musical development of the country, and a host of other injuries to music, in its artistic manifestations, by virtue — or rather by vice — of the multiplication of the various music-making machines.[29]

Here's another example, something less benign. Beginning in the early 1930s, some medical professionals became infatuated with the idea of using radiation therapies for a wide range of ailments. The strategy became an international phenomenon and continued right into the 1950s. A Vancouver woman lost two of her brothers when they died of cancer in their forties. Both men had had their chests and necks irradiated when they were babies in the belief that it would prevent crib death.

Doctors also believed radiation was a safe and effective procedure for treating inflamed tonsils and adenoids in toddlers. They didn't know the radiation would be blamed for causing some cancers years later, nor did

it a "religion." For a somewhat expanded version of Nye's sublime, for example, see Dora Russell's *The Religion of the Machine Age* (London: Routledge and Kegan Paul, 1983). "Idolatry of the machine, the wrongful and now evil use of its powers, is destroying human life and happiness and will make an end of all life on our earth" (p. 255). The book is notable for several reasons. Maybe the most compelling is that Russell first undertook the project in 1920, when she started to write the book and received a publishing contract from Routledge and Kegan Paul. For a variety of reasons she abandoned it, only to pick it up again close to six decades later, completing it in 1982 at age 86 and seeing it published with its original publisher.

26. "Last year,

they understand that the organ they regarded as a hazard to health — the thymus — is essential to good health. . . .

It was an era when people were enamoured with new machines and technology, and everyone was in awe of radiology equipment. "I remember getting my feet x-rayed in the shoe department at Woodward's as a child," recalled Dr. Anne Junker, a professor of infectious diseases and immunology at the University of BC and BC Children's Hospital.[30]

It is certainly true that every new tool has repercussive effects, and adopting new technologies always means displacing something. Sometimes the displacements are intended and explicit, other times they are tangential, incremental and/or ironic. Take the case of pesticides and antibiotics, which were designed to eliminate specific menaces from agricultural or human systems. We are now witnessing a phenomenal growth in pesticide- and drug-resistant organisms, many of which are far more dangerous than the original problem. In "solving" one problem, we find the revenge/rebound effects are proving themselves equally (and perhaps much more) problematic.

People are often baffled by technology and ascribe to new tools all kinds of absurd uses or deliberately ignore possible consequences. As Edward Tenner points out in *Why Things Bite Back: Technology and the Revenge of Unintended Consequences,*

Something else was happening as disasters were coming under control in the West. The very means of preventing them sometimes created the risk of even larger ones in the future. And, even more significant, the gradual, long-term, dispersed problem proved far less tractable than the sudden, shocking one. As we shall see, the steady seepage of petroleum products from small industrial, residential, and service station tanks became a more serious problem than any of the great oil spills.[31]

There is something prophetic about this. Sometimes the consequences of technology are immediate and obvious: using the spell-check on this machine likely makes me a less capable editor and speller. Cars all over the roads make bike riding less popular (and less safe) and contribute heavily to the greenhouse effect. Other kinds of consequences are more subtle and subjective: the popularity of television reduces community interactions; microwaves degrade the experience of cooking. Still other consequences are long term and can only be understood over the span of many years. For example, irradiating babies frequently has disastrous effects on their health later in life, but it seemed like a good idea at the time.

26,893 new food and household products materialized on store shelves around the world, including 115 deodorants, 187 breakfast cereals and 303 women's fragrances." *Globe and Mail*, March 1, 2005, p. A18.

27. Neil Postman, *Technopoly* (New York: Knopf, 1992), p. 28.

28. Takis Fotopoulos, "Towards," in *Democracy and Nature*, 4, no. 1, issue 10, p. 86.

29. Daniel Boorstin, *The Americans: The Democratic Experience* (New York: Vintage, 1974), p. 657, quoted in Gordon Graham, *The Internet:// a philosophical inquiry* (London: Routledge, 1999).

30. *Vancouver Sun*, February 9, 2001, p. A1.

31. Edward Tenner, *Why*

In the early years of virtual hysteria, many touted the Internet as the saviour of our culture. Cyberspace was utopia, or at least the apex of civilized communication. Howard Rheingold claimed that electronic communication represented the greatest resource ever for community-building. "The future of the net is connected to the future of community, democracy, education, science and intellectual life."[32] Not to be outdone, Daniel Burstein and David Kline proclaimed that the development of cyberspace meant that "civilization now stands at one of those great historic junctures that arise only a few times in a millennium,"[33] while Derrick de Kerckhove claimed that what he calls "webness" "will bring about enough contradictions to require a fundamental psychological restructuring of our connected and personal minds."[34]

Oh really?

△

We rarely see new tools as antagonistic to culture, but often ascribe levelling characteristics to technology; that is to say, new tools are often presumed to democratize and liberate. As Daniel Boorstin,

Things Bite Back (New York: Knopf, 1997), p. 24.

32. Howard Rheingold, *The Virtual Community* (Reading, MA: William Patrick, 1993), p. 6.

33. Daniel Burstein, and David Kline, *Road War-*

eminent historian and Librarian of Congress, wrote in 1978:

> *Technology dilutes and dissolves ideology. . . . Technology is the natural foe of nationalism.*
>
> *Broadcasting is perhaps the most potent everyday witness to the converging powers of technology. The most democratic of all forms of public communication, broadcasting converges people, drawing them into the same experiences in ways never before possible.*
>
> *The democratizing impact of television has been strikingly similar to the historic impact of printing. Even in this, television's first half-century, we have seen its power to disband armies, cashier presidents, to create a whole new democratic world — democratic in ways never before imagined, even in America.*[35]

It sounds ridiculous — television or the Internet creating a new democratic world — but this is a sentiment that legitimately exists.[36] If everyone is invited to join in, isn't that democracy?

At one time the Internet was widely lauded as "democratic" or a "tool for democracy." See, for one example, *Time Magazine*'s special 1995 issue on "cyberspace": "In a world already too divided against itself — rich against poor, producer against consumer — cyberspace offers the nearest thing to a level playing field."[37] Not many folks want to make that claim today. The net is a complicated and complicating tool, useful for much, trivial in many ways, and not much of a leveller in any real sense.

John B. Thompson, writing just before the Internet deluge, describes the changing definitions of the public and specifically points to "*global scrutiny . . .* political leaders must now act in an arena which is in principle open to view on a global scale."[38] Importantly that doesn't mean decentralized *power*. There is little reason to think that a population with global information at its fingertips will be more active in its own affairs. If that were true, the television would have significantly increased democratic discourse. Having access to an ever-increasing flow of information is just that, and not a lot more.

While it is hard to imagine genuine dispersions of power in today's political scenario, knowledge must be among the preconditions for possible fundamental change. But can information, per se, be named knowledge? If so, then should not the omnipresence of television and its massive dissemination of information create massive democratic possibility?

Maybe, but knowing about something doesn't mean you can do anything about it. As Gordon Graham says, "The fact that we know

riors (New York: Dutton, 1995), p. 1.

34. Derrick de Kerckhove, *Connected Intelligence* (Toronto: Somerville House Publishers, 1997), p. xxiii.

35. Daniel Boorstin, *The Republic of Technology* (New York: Harper and Row, 1978), pp. 6–7.

36. See, for one of many examples, Howard Frederick, "Networks and the Emergence of Global Civil Society," in *Global Networks*, Linda Haraim, ed. (Cambridge, MA: MIT Press, 1994). "The world is truly moving into a 'new order'. The age of democracy may have had its beginnings in the French and American revolutions, but only today is it finally reaching the hearts and minds of sympathetic

more may bring us to a greater realization of how little control we have, which is why I say that 'knowledge is frustration' is an equal contender with the more familiar claim that 'knowledge is power'."[39]

Lewis Mumford has drawn distinctions between what he terms "authoritarian and democratic technics." "Democracy, in the primal sense I shall use the term, is necessarily most visible in small communities and groups, whose members meet frequently face to face, interact freely and are known to each other as persons."[40] Beyond that, he argues, technologies represent a tension either toward or away from democracy:

> My thesis, to put it bluntly, is that from late Neolithic times in the Near East, right down to our own day, two technologies have recurrently existed side by side: one authoritarian, the other democratic, the first system-centered, immensely powerful, but inherently unstable, the other man-centered, relatively weak, but resourceful and durable.[41]

If it is true that some technologies are inherently authoritarian, perhaps some tools are built for domination. Or maybe it is the culture that is constructed around domination and tools are only tools. One way or the other it is important to acknowledge the relationship between technology and imperialism. Daniel Headrick opened his book on the subject by writing:

> Among the many important events of the nineteenth century, two were of momentous consequence for the entire world. One was the progress and power of industrial technology; the other was the domination and exploitation of Africa and much of Asia by Europeans.[42]

The dialectical relationship between technological advances and the domination of non-Western cultures is a complex one, but there can be no question that the huge burst of imperialist force that erupted in the mid to late 1800s and continues today has been significantly aided and abetted by technology.

As Headrick points out, imperialism has been a triumph of "vaccines and napalm, of ships and aircraft, of electricity and radio, of plastics and printing presses.[43] Without new tools, new conquests were doomed or possibly never even imagined. The ideology of colonization was certainly in place regardless of technological innovation, but breechloaders, quinine, steamships and many other inventions made the physical reality possible, and the successes then spurred new innovation.

The idea of new tools has also always been closely tied to ideals

populations around the world. This 'preferred' world order of democratic change depends heavily on the efficiency of communications systems" (p. 294).

37. Quoted in John Goyder, *Technology and Society: A Canadian Perspective* (Peterborough, ON: Broadview, 1997), p. 175.

38. John B. Thompson, *The Media and Modernity* (Stanford, CA: Stanford University Press, 1995), p. 148. See also Thompson's *Ideology and Modern Culture* (Stanford, CA: Stanford University Press, 1991).

39. Graham, *The Internet*, p. 34.

40. Lewis Mumford, "Authoritarian and Democratic Technics," in *Technology and Culture*, Melvin Kranzberg and William Davenport, eds. (New York: Schocken, 1972), p. 51.

41. Ibid., p. 52.

of freedom and individual possibility, the liberation from natural bonds reconfigured and technically achievable. As Heather Menzies writes, citing George Grant,

> The moral discourse of "values" and "freedom" is not independent of the will to technology, but a language fashioned in the same forge together with the will to technology. Fused and transformed, old-fashioned virtues become technically phrased: certain technical procedures and precautions which are prescribed as the ethical way of doing genetic-engineering research for example. Freedom is technically measured in conquests of time and space.[44]

So can more technology make us more free, or are there thresholds where technology makes us less free? Or are certain kinds of technology just trouble? Is it a quantity or quality issue, or both? For example, is the proliferation of cars the issue, or do we just need bio-diesel or hydrogen cars? Are the answers to technological problems inevitably more (and maybe better) technology? Ivan Illich argues, in *Energy and Equity*, against the automobile and for limits to speed. His analysis is particularly useful here, especially with a perspective informed by the more than thirty years since it was written. Illich makes the simple point that there is a threshold after which speed slows us down, when the pursuit of *private* speed is a net *public* loss.

> Past a certain speed threshold, the transportation industry dictates the configuration of social space. Motorways expand, driving wedges between neighbours and removing fields beyond the distance a farmer can walk. Ambulances take clinics beyond the few miles a sick child can be carried. The doctor will no longer come to the house, because vehicles have made the hospital into the right place to be sick. Once heavy lorries reach a village high in the Andes, part of the local market disappears. Later, when the high school arrives at the plaza along with the paved highway, more and more of the young people move to the city, until not one family is left which does not long for a reunion with someone hundreds of miles away, down the coast . . .
>
> Beyond a critical speed, no one can save time without forcing another to lose it . . . Beyond a certain speed, motorized vehicles create remoteness which they alone can shrink.[45]

42. Daniel Headrick, *The Tools of Empire: Technology and European Imperialism in the Nineteenth Century* (New York: Oxford University Press, 1981), p. 3.

43. Ibid., p. 4.

44. Heather Menzies, *Fast Forward and Out of Control* (Toronto: Macmillan, 1989), p. 50.

45. Ivan Illich, *Energy and Equity* (New York: Harper and Row, 1974), pp. 23, 30.

THE OPPOSITE OF ADVENTURE

In the new IT world, conventional and parochial ties are shed in favour of a penultimate kind of freedom to go where you please, when you please and with whom you please. Social interactions are maintained only when useful or interesting. These are very basic and vernacularly understood assumptions about Internet culture, and they all suggest, implicitly and explicitly, a sense of risk, adventure and exciting exploration.

While an image of reckless and spontaneous adventure continues to surround virtual discourse, there is a simultaneous obsession with safety and security online. Nowhere in non-military life is there more talk of conspiracies, government intrusion in citizen affairs, the coding of messages, the security of credit card numbers, the possibilities of personal information falling into the wrong hands, etc. There remains a widespread distrust of purchasing consumer goods via the Internet using a credit card, for example. At the same time, most people are totally unafraid to hand their credit card to a waiter, who then disappears with it for five minutes. The actual risk of having a card number stolen online can hardly be greater than that of having it copied by a clerk, yet virtuality engenders more fear and suspicion.

One of the ironic tendencies of virtuality is just this: while it promises an adventurous frontierism, evoking images of hiking in the backcountry, white-water kayaking and rappelling across glaciers, the Internet's real appeal and power lie in the reverse, its cocooning vision of safety and security. Online, one can go anywhere without having to actually travel, meet people freely without worrying about who they might be, talk dirty with clean hands, shop without having to brave the crowds, chat with friends without having to see them. It is a territory bent on eradicating risk, where one can come and go without responsibility and never worry about leaving home or even the chair. It is about flattening and controlling the surprises of lived life, the opposite of adventure, and our best extension thus far of the home-as-castle vision.

This points to a similarly understood irony of contemporary culture. While the transcendence of physical limits is the basis of the Internet's power, the defeat of time and space results in a sharp decline in the possibility of public space, not its promised revival. Spending time online is not about being in the public sphere, and while surfing the web is mostly like cruising a mall, the total experience of the Internet is a new postmodern kind of space: open yet

non-public, privatized yet not fully owned. As Martha Rosler put it when speaking of new urban frontiers and homelessness,

> Post-modern discontinuity, like scattered sites of industrial and image production, is also manifested as a blurring of the boundaries between public and private life. . . . Intentionally or not, this blurring serves the interest of greater but less confrontational social control.
>
> Contemporary society, with its changes in information and transportation flows that have forced a de jure adherence to social ideals of equal participation — not least in consumerism — but without adequate economic means to put them into practise, no longer supports that late version of a chain of being in which each being holds a particular, known place.[46]

46. Martha Rosler, "Fragments of a Metropolitan Viewpoint," in *If You Lived Here*, B. Wallis, ed. (Seattle: Bay Press, 1991), p. 17.

Spending time on the web really is a lot like cruising a superhighway, and it feels about as much like the public sphere as a freeway does, or as conducive to genuine public discourse as a mall. In many ways, a shopping mall is especially useful as a metaphor for considering the easy blurring of public and private.

Like all decent-sized malls, the Internet claims to contain everything, to represent and recreate the whole world, only better and cleaner. Carefully constructed, mall culture is limitless and attempts to satisfy every potential consumer. Speaking about the West Edmonton Mall, Margaret Crawford writes:

> At the opening ceremony aboard the Santa Maria, one of the mall's developers, Nader Ghermezian, shouted in triumph, "What we have done means you don't have to go to New York or Paris or Disneyland or Hawaii. We have it all here for you in one place, in Edmonton, Alberta, Canada!" Publicity for the Fantasyland Hotel asks "What country do you want to sleep in tonight?" — offering theme rooms based not only on faraway places such as Polynesia and Hollywood, and distant times such as ancient Rome and Victorian England, but also on modes of transportation, from horse-drawn carriages to pickup trucks. [47]

This is exactly the fantasyland the Internet has positioned itself as, only on a larger, more malleable and intrusive level. Not surprisingly, the visceral sense you get surfing the net is almost exactly what you get when cruising a mall — a twitchy, distracted sense of both hyperreality and stupor.

> For Joan Didion the mall is an addictive environmental drug, where "one moves for a while in aqueous suspension, not only of light, but of judgement, not only of judgement but of personality". . . . William Kowinski identified mal de mall as a perceptual paradox brought on by simultaneous stimulation and sedation, characterized by disorientation, anxiety and apathy. [48]

In this context, what appears to be and is perceived as generally public space is really privately owned and governed, and mall security can legally eject anyone who is inferring with the consumer agenda. [49]

Michael Sorkin has nicely named this "the Disneyfication of culture," and in many ways Disney, and especially Disneyland, are the real spiritual basis for both mall and net culture. The constant simulations, all referencing other, physically distant people or places, and the necessary abstractions of authenticity are the elements of living fantasy. [50] Writing in 1992, well before the Internet explosion, Sorkin drew the connection:

> The urbanism of Disneyland is precisely the urbanism of universal equivalence. In this new city, the idea of distinct places is dispersed into a sea of universal placelessness as everyplace becomes destination and any

47. Margaret Crawford, "The World in a Shopping Mall," in Variations on a Theme Park, Michael Sorkin, ed. (New York: Noonday, 1992), p. 4.

48. Ibid., p. 14.

49. As a man in Albany, New York, found out in March 2003 when he refused to take off his "Give Peace A Chance" T-shirt and was arrested and taken away in handcuffs. The man "said police tried to convince him he was wrong in his actions by refusing to remove the T-shirt because the mall 'was like a private house and . . . [he] was acting poorly.'" "Man Arrested for Peace T-shirt" reported on CNN.com, March 5, 2003 (cnn.com/2003/US/Northeast/03/04/iraq.usa.shirt.reut/).

50. Or as Marie-Laure Ryan wrote in "Cyberspace, Virtuality and the Text," "The

destination can be anyplace. The world of traditional urban arrangements is colonized by the penetration of a new multinational corridor, leading always to a single human subject, the monadic consumer. The ultimate consequence is likely to be the increasing irrelevance of actual movement and the substitution of the even more completely artificial reality of electronic "virtual" space.[51]

In the early 1970s, historian William Irwin Thompson spoke of Disneyland as a "shattered landscape in which the individual moves through a world of discontinuities: Mississippi riverboats, medieval castles, and rocket ships equally fill the reality of a single moment."[52] The discontinuity is essential, because in the absence of place, alternatives flow in easily. Theme parks, Disney and virtuality are capable of providing titillating and pleasing possibilities at the drop of a hat and naming them as safe and enjoyable fun, without all the worry, unpredictability and messiness.

visitors of Disneyland are more thrilled by automata performing as pirates or animals in the jungle than they would be by real animals or by role-playing humans." In *Cyberspace Textuality: Computer Technology and Literary Theory*, Marie-Laure Ryan, ed. (Bloomington: Indiana University Press, 1999), p. 90.

51. Michael Sorkin, "See You in Disneyland," in *Variations on a Theme Park*, Michael Sorkin, ed. (New York: Noonday, 1992), p. 217.

52. Quoted in Jeffrey Meikle, *American Plastic: A Cultural History* (New Brunswick, NJ; Rutgers University Press, 1995), p. 280.

Come

Join

Our

Team!

134

CHAPTER NINE

A World Out Of Control?

Policing, Common Space and

Gentrification

I have never seen a situation so dismal that a policeman couldn't make it worse.

BRENDAN BEHAN

1. I am sticking closely and explicitly in this chapter to the issue of policing at the community level. I am speaking specifically about the interaction between the police and everyday people every day.

2. For more on this see, for example, George Mosse, *Police Forces in History* (London: Sage Publications, 1975).

When talk turns to safety, most people immediately think of crime and subsequently the police. However, it is critical to understand the police in a wider context, as just one piece in a mosaic of security institutions. In particular, I want to link the community experience of policing to a broad (and broadening) apparatus that defines safety as keeping power in place: *maintaining order*. It is worth exploring the line of thinking that conflates policing with safety, and whether or not that makes much sense in a local context,[1] and how our understanding of the role of police is governed by our conceptions and expectations of safety. More specifically, I want to link our understanding of security to gentrification and the regulation of everyday space.

The omnipresent modern police force is perceived as having always been with us, like school, but, also like school, comprehensive police forces are actually a relatively recent invention, first emerging in London in 1829 when Robert Peel established the Metropolitan Police Force.[2] A professionalized police force responsible for maintaining all public order is not immutable. Certainly some kind of collective response to crime is necessary lest the maintenance of security descend into fiefdoms of private armies, personal police forces and guarded manors: but ironically that, in some ways, is exactly what our urban environments look like now.

YOU'RE WITH US OR AGAINST US

A few years ago I became involved in our neighbourhood residents' council[3] and was surprised (although in retrospect it was pretty predictable) by the degree to which opinions about police fundamentally divide us. People assume that local community councils are most effective when they deal with small-scale, very local concerns, and this means they tend to focus on minor crime: break-and-enter, drug dealing, drinking in the park, graffiti and intimidation. Not surprisingly, these concerns often cause residents' organizations to zero in on youth, especially kids of colour, and overwhelmingly the concerns are vocalized most articulately and noisily by middle-class adults.

Many of our meetings broke up rancorously, with members reduced to sniping back and forth about the cops and safety. Some people argued that we needed more police in the neighbourhood because crime was increasing and the wave of lawlessness needed to be pushed back. Others argued that the police were part of the problem and cited incidents of police harassment and violence. Inevitably, each claim came with the assertion that "Things are changing," becoming less safe than they were before.

These arguments have been echoed in the Vancouver media over the past few years, around the issue of street people, squeegee kids and panhandling. Actually there's rarely much debate, mostly complaints about poor people. In August 2006, just as I was finishing this book up, for example, the *Vancouver Sun* ran a huge front page headline: "Beggars, Drug Dealers Kill Convention Business."[4] The line is a familiar one: things are getting much, much worse, and something has to be done.

> *Aggressive panhandlers and drug dealers are damaging Vancouver's international reputation as a safe tourist destination, the leaders of the City's $10-billion tourism industry warn.*
>
> *The situation has become so dire that beggars and drug dealers have even been accosting tourists inside the gilded bathrooms of the landmark Fairmont Hotel Vancouver.*
>
> *Distressed by their experiences in dealing with pushy panhandlers upon arriving in the city, convention planners are now choosing to take their business elsewhere, said the general manager of the Hotel Vancouver. . . .*
>
> *The Downtown Vancouver Business Improvement Association estimates Vancouver hotels have lost contracts worth $500,000.*
>
> *Philip Barnes, general manager of the Hotel Vancouver, said guests*

3. A local elected council intended to represent community concerns and act as a forum for local discussion.

4. Ironically, the article was illustrated with a photo of a guy sitting on the pavement obsequiously holding his hat out, well out of the way of people on the sidewalk. It looked the opposite of "aggressive panhandling."

regularly tell him they are "stunned" and "scared" by the panhandling and aggressive behaviour on the streets near the hotel at night.

"I've lived on four continents and in six countries, including two cities known at the time for their crime rates: New York and Houston," said Barnes. "The problem is more acute in this city now. I never went through the aggressive panhandling and the drug activities in New York in the 1980s as I see now."[5]

There are in fact a lot of panhandlers on the streets of Vancouver, but the *Sun* identifies them as a crime problem requiring an aggressive police solution, not as poor people requiring social action. The analysis is a familiar one, separating behaviour from the contexts that create it. As Philip Barnes of the Hotel Vancouver said in the article, "This is not about the poor, about people on the street because of mental illness or other legitimate reasons."[6] Who does he think panhandlers are?

As anti-poverty activist Jean Swanson responded in a letter that the newspaper printed the next day, fifteen years ago the city had poor, homeless, mentally ill and drug-addicted people, but fewer street people. In the interim, welfare rules have been changed so that many people are unable to qualify, the rates themselves have been slashed significantly, and affordable housing programs have essentially disappeared. Swanson writes that addressing those problems is the only effective way to address the issue of aggressive panhandling. "You can attack impoverished people endlessly, but they still have to eat and sleep. It would be more humane and efficient to change the policies causing the problems."[7]

It is hardly a surprise that the *Vancouver Sun* is all over street people in the wake of an *Economist* report reviewing the city's downtown,

Homeless panhandlers yell at theatre-goers, while young addicts deal drugs on street corners. They spill out from the Downtown East Side, an area of decrepit boarding houses, sleazy bars and boarded-up shops infamous for the country's highest rates of poverty and drug addiction. Its ills have resisted decades of expensive government effort. ... If Vancouver is to continue to live up to its reputation as an urban paradise, it will need a city government with the power, as well as the will, to keep it that way.[8]

That one small paragraph has produced a paroxysm of hand-wringing and calls for a sturdier police response. By ignoring the context of the problem, it became easy to morph complex social issues into a simple "us vs. them," we-need-more-cops-being-more-aggressive response. This is not the same as saying crime or harass-

5. Gwen Preston "Beggars, Drug Dealers Kill Convention Business," *Vancouver Sun*, August 18, 2006. p. A1.

6. Ibid., p. A2.

7. Jean Swanson, "Politicians have to deal with shadow cast over city," *Vancouver Sun*, August 19, 2006, p. C3.

8. "Growing Pains: A great city more troubled than it is cracked up to be," *The Economist*, July 6, 2006.

ment by homeless people is all right; but not dealing with the root causes of impoverishment is really being "soft on crime."

Interestingly, that same *Vancouver Sun* produced an editorial three days later considering the current Canadian Justice Minister's suggestion that kids as young as 10 who break the law should be dealt with by the adult criminal justice system. The minister, Vic Toews suggested that "We need to give the courts jurisdiction to intervene in the lives of these young people," and the editorial response was a surprisingly incisive one:

> *It's tempting to think that the law can solve all social problems, but in reality law enforcement is merely an after-the-fact response to problematic behaviour. Indeed if the child welfare system were able to provide all necessary treatment programs, Toews himself would have to admit that there would be little left for the courts to do.*[9]

That's exactly correct. Now extend that same analysis to include panhandlers, drug addiction, and poverty-driven crime, and let's stop baying about crime being out of control, and let's stop pretending that cops can solve our most pressing social concerns.

CRIME DOWN, ANXIETY UP?

If you were only to read daily newspapers or watch network TV it would be easy to think that crime is out of control in Canada, that people are afraid to step out outside. As Prime Minister Stephen Harper put it shortly after his 2006 election, affirming that fighting crime was a key Conservative Party plank:

> *They've [Canadians] told us they want to be able to go about their daily lives without having to worry about getting hit by a stray bullet fired by a gang member. Or being killed by a street racer losing control of his stolen vehicle.*
>
> *They've told us they want to get real on crime. And they want to put an end to gang, gun and drug violence. They want us to walk the walk – not just talk the talk. Canadians have told us they want action now – not more talk.*
>
> *And that's what we're going to do.*[10]

But that's not what Canadians have been saying at all. The Treasury Board of Canada's Secretariat, in its *Canada's Performance Report 2005*, confirmed this:

9. "At-risk children better served by social workers than the courts," *Vancouver Sun* editorial, August 22, 2006, p. A10.
10. John Gray, "Tough Choices About Tough Justice," *CBC Online*, April 6, 2006, www.cbc.ca/news/background/realitycheck/20060406gray.html

According to the 2004 General Social Survey, 94.0 per cent of Canadians were satisfied that they were personally safe from becoming a victim. This proportion was up from 86.0 per cent in 1993 and 91.0 per cent in 1999. Overall, 95.0 per cent of men were satisfied that they were personally safe from becoming a victim, compared with 93.0 per cent of women. This gap between sexes is narrowing as the proportion for women rose by five percentage points between 1999 and 2004, while the proportion for men went up two points.

In 2004, 58.0 per cent of people believed that there had been no change in crime levels, while 30.0 per cent felt that crime had worsened over the previous five years. These views were fairly consistent with those reported in the 1999 survey. These perceptions on neighbourhood crime have improved, however, since the 1993 survey, when Canadians were more likely to say crime was on the rise. At that time, 46.0 per cent felt it had increased.[11]

The cold reality of crime in Canada is that it is declining. Stats Canada figures published July 2006 by the Canadian Centre for Justice Statistics include:

- The overall crime rate dropped 5 percent in 2005.
- The national crime rate had increased during the 1960s, 70s, and 80s, peaking in 1991. Crime rates then fell throughout the rest of the 1990s, stabilizing somewhat in the early 2000s.
- Declines in crime rates were observed in all provinces and territories. The largest provincial drops were reported in Manitoba (-8 percent), New Brunswick (-8 percent), and Saskatchewan (-6 percent).
- Drug offences decreased for the second time in three years, dropping 6 percent. Cannabis offences accounted for the majority of drug offences, and fell 12 percent.
- The youth crime rate, as measured by the number of youths formally charged plus youths cleared by means other than the laying of a charge, dropped 6 percent. Youth violent crime dropped 2 percent, while youth property crime was down 12 percent.[12]

Much of the current wave of fear-mongering about crime has been driven by a widely publicized series of homicides and gun incidents in Toronto in the summer of 2005. The situation was definitely troubling, and fueled by a certain amount of racial profiling and questionable attitudes towards Caribbean immigrants, Toronto-based national media whipped up a titillated frenzy that

11. Treasury Board of Canada Secretariat, "Canada's Social Foundations: Safe and Secure Communities" in Annex 3: Indicators and Additional Information of *Canada's Performance 2005* (Ottawa: Author, 2005). Available online at www.tbs-sct. gc.ca/report/gov-rev/05/ann302_ e.asp#11

12. Marie Gannon, "Crime Statistics in Canada, 2005" Juristat, 26, no. 4 (July 2006), www.statcan. ca/english/ freepub/85-002-XIE/85-002-XIE2006004.pdf.

Ontario was crime-infested, and Toronto specifically was dubbed "Murder City." But in 2005 Ontario had (you guessed it) the lowest crime rate of any province in Canada, way less than half that of Saskatchewan, way less even than BC for that matter.[13]

So why are Stephen Harper, the Conservative Party and media fixating on crime? Is it just that it is spectacular and makes for good headlines? Or that violence tends to inflame people's passions? It makes sense when police associations or car-alarm companies or home-defence system manufacturers talk about crime as out of control: that's just good business. But why does that story continue to resonate, even when we know it isn't true?

COMMUNITY POLICING, POLICING THE COMMUNITY

There is a popular park right in the middle of my neighbourhood. It has a great playground, a wading pool, tennis courts and some grassy areas. It is constantly full of kids and families. It is also frequented by local teens, hippies smoking blunts, drug-dealing types, people crashed out in the grass, dog owners throwing balls to their pooches, folks congregating under trees, dopes playing hacky sack. The park reflects the neighbourhood demographic pretty accurately. It is certainly complex and contested space.

A few years ago a battle ensued when the city decided to place a community police office (CPO) right in the middle of the park, in what was once the caretaker's building. For many months there was a lively and sometimes heated debate at community forums, in local papers and on the street. In the end, with the support of an organized homeowners' association and the community centre, the office was installed.

The winning argument was that the park should be a place for kids, that it was a place we were losing, and that something had to be done. The office was to be a community operation, run by volunteers, with no permanent police presence. And if you aren't doing something illegal, why are you worried?

One of the opposing arguments was that a police station would not solve any problems; it would only move them around. The main Vancouver police station, for example, is in the middle of one of the most crime-ridden and poverty-stricken areas of Canada, the Downtown Eastside, and has proved totally unable to solve crime there. Unsurprisingly, the CPO has not "solved" crime in the park either.

There is now a much heavier police presence in the park, with

13. Ibid.

teams of volunteers regularly cruising around, but crime has *not* been reduced. Illegal activity is perhaps a little more surreptitious, but no one in the area claims that there is significantly less crime. More than that, the activity that the office was specifically intended to address – drug and alcohol use — has not declined. Some of it has just moved up the street to the next park, the one across the street from my house. Now this second park is filled with drinkers and smokers. Another neighbourhood group wants to clean up this park too, failing to note that the original park policing project never delivered on the promises made for it — it has failed to make the neighbourhood any safer.

Or has it failed? The introduction of a police presence into community conversations about public space transforms social issues into battles where the language and terms of reference can be militarized. The effect is to take complicated conversations and turn them into arguments that can be won or lost, reducing complex social problems to the winning or losing of common space: taking back the park.

Thus community safety becomes an issue of Whose side are you on? and policing becomes a class signifier that ignores the complex matrix of social relationships that create tensions in the park, reducing them to: *Are you for drug dealers, or for children?* Policing begets more policing. Police embody the dialectics of confrontation, and when confrontation occurs, the response is to call for more police. The treatment creates the symptoms it is supposed to treat. Maybe the CPO has succeeded, and the community has become one step further removed from dealing with the context and causes of the problem.

There are many useful suggestions for demilitarizing police forces and making them accountable to the communities they ostensibly serve[14] — for example, getting cops out of their cars and having them walk their patrols, getting rid of their guns, making them report to local citizen boards, replacing local police beats with citizen patrols, etc. Unfortunately, police unions tend to be strong, well-connected and well-organized, and they can destroy the political careers of those who get in their way. They also tend to reflexively rely on the same arguments: "We're keeping you safe and we need every possible resource and power. Anything that gets in our way is tantamount to supporting crime and danger." It is a self-sustaining and very effective argument. Question police power and you might as well be raping old ladies yourself.

This logic often reduces community policing, however well-intentioned or bucolic it might sound, to middle-class people

14. Some that I have found useful include Paul Chavigny, *Edge of the Knife: Police Violence in the Americas* (New York: New Press, 1995); Frank Donner, *Protectors of Privilege: Red Squads and Police Oppression in Urban America* (Berkeley: University of California Press, 1990); Mark Findlay and Ugljesa Zvekic, eds., *Alternative Policing Styles: Cross-Cultural Perspectives* (Boston: Kluwer Law and Taxation Publishers, 1993); Larry Gaines and Gary Cordner, eds., *Policing Perspectives: An Anthology* (Los Angeles:

WATCH YOURSELF

Roxbury, 1999);
Susan Miller, *Gender and Community Policing: Walking the Talk* (Boston: Northeastern University Press, 1999); Jill Nelson, ed., *Police Brutality: An Anthology* (New York: Norton, 2000) and Brian Williams, *Citizen Perspectives on Community Policing: A Case Study in Athens, Georgia* (Albany: SUNY Press, 1998).

wandering around in orange vests, calling the cops when they see something they don't like. Using the rhetoric and language of safety, community members become extensions of the police, volunteers doing the dirty work and marketing it as community safety, based on the assumption that NIMBY homeowners are the rightful arbiters of public space. It is in this that police are perhaps most effective, increasing the scope of their influence through indirect means. Community safety offices and neighbourhood policing are potentially useful tools, but they have to answer to the community and all citizens, not the police or already privileged interests.

YOU'LL GET YOURS

All too often, conversations around policing and personal safety are stripped of context, but security is always contingent and politicized. That is to say, violence, frustration, and crime can best be dealt with by understanding the soil from which they emerge. That's not excusing violence, but being rational about it.

In December 2001, Robert Fisk, a British-born reporter, was

driving near the Afghan-Pakistan border when he was attacked. He was beaten badly by an angry mob and barely survived with the aid of luck and the grace of some fortunate and unasked-for assistance.

15. Robert Fisk, "My Beating by Refugees Is a Symbol of the Hatred and Fury of This Filthy War," *The Independent*, December 10, 2001.

I couldn't blame them for what they were doing. In fact, if I were the Afghan refugees of Kila Abdullah, close to the Afghan-Pakistan border, I would have done just the same to Robert Fisk. Or any other Westerner I could find.

So why record my few minutes of terror and self-disgust under assault near the Afghan border, bleeding and crying like an animal, when hundreds — let us be frank and say thousands — of innocent civilians are dying under American air strikes in Afghanistan, when the "War of Civilisation" is burning and maiming the Pashtuns of Kandahar and destroying their homes because "good" must triumph over "evil"? . . .

All the Afghan men and boys who had attacked me who should never have done so but whose brutality was entirely the product of others, of us — of we who had armed their struggle against the Russians and ignored their pain and laughed at their civil war and then armed and paid them again for the "War for Civilisation" just a few miles away and then bombed their homes and ripped up their families and called them "collateral damage."[15]

Fisk's report of his experiences brought a cascade of howls from the conservative media, which called him anti-American, a hater of the West, a traitor, the worst kind of liberal, weak-kneed relativist, all because he refused to blame his attackers and was able to contextualize the situation.

Getting attacked, beaten up, robbed, taken advantage of or mistreated always sucks, and the immediate gut-level response is often to reach out and hurt someone back; we want revenge and retribution. In most cases, though, we are able to step back, consider the context, think things through and acknowledge that, sometimes, we were asking for it.

That's the title of a tremendously powerful personal essay published in *Granta 68: Love Stories*. James Hamilton-Paterson was a young Brit working in Libya in 1966. One day he took a car and drove well out of Tripoli and along the coast. He found a secluded beach to suntan on and, while resting, was surrounded by five Bedouins who subdued him, holding a huge rock over his head menacingly. He was then raped repeatedly.

It was excessively painful and disagreeable, and it seemed to last rather longer than forever. Not once but five times, the men democratically moving around and taking over the rock in turn. . . . There is no point in dwelling on the agonizing drive back into town, the gore on the upholstery, the final humiliation of being examined by a roguish Yugoslav doctor in the old Italian hospital on the seafront (Ah, my friend, it is spring!).

In time, he discovered that as horrible as the experience had been, it hadn't caused irreparable damage, emotionally or physically, and he came to see it as one of those things that happen. Very, very bad luck, but bad luck with a lesson.

In a metaphorical sense, though, I surely had been asking for it by so cockily failing to take politics into account. . . . My rapists, it seemed, had been committing a political more than an erotic act. I was violated because I was a white foreign male. I was not even a person but an object to be despised and humiliated. In my youthful British arrogance I had believed I was exempt from being thought anything other than benignly apolitical, and could in any case never be taken for an American. I had failed to read the signs and paid for my stupidity.[16]

This is not to say (nor am I implying) that rape is ever justified anywhere, but Hamilton-Paterson's response was similar to Fisk's: abhorring his own pain and suffering while acknowledging how the circumstances shaped events. Even the *9/11 Commission Report* was clear in this regard:

When people lose hope, when societies break down, when countries fragment, the breeding grounds for terrorism are created. . . . Economic and political liberties tend to be linked.[17]

Sometimes things happen to people that are not good or justifiable, but they have to be put into some kind of context. If you walk into a poor neighbourhood brandishing a Rolex, maybe you deserve to get jacked. Ostentatiously flashing wealth around people who have very little is considered provocation, and few will shed a tear for you. If you are a traveller in a poor country spending wads of money extravagantly, maybe you deserve to get robbed. Everyone who has travelled in a poor country knows this. If you get your backpack stolen out of your room in a poverty-stricken place, it sucks for sure, but that's part of the deal.

This reality is universally understood. It is also true on a global level, which explains why a New Mexico company can market "Going Canadian" packets to American travellers, on the assumption that Canadian travellers are less likely to be targeted than

16. James Hamilton-Paterson, "Asking for It," *Granta* 68 (December 1999), pp. 230-31.

17. Quoted in James Baker and Warren Christopher, "There Are Other Ways To Keep America Safe," originally from the Washington Post, reprinted in the *Honolulu Advertiser*, December 20, 2004, p. A10.

"ugly Americans." For US$24.95 you can purchase a Canadian flag T-shirt, lapel pin, sticker and patch for a backpack along with a booklet with Canadian info and helpful tips on being a Canuck in case you are questioned.[18]

18. See the T-Shirt King website (t-shirtking.com).

It is not that Americans, or Canadians or Europeans, are necessarily imperialists. We are people, not ambassadors for our countries nor representatives of their foreign policies. On the other hand, we all recognize the wealth, privilege and injustice that we represent and the arrogance of our travelling. In a world beset with mind-boggling inequities, brandishing our wealth in the faces of those who have so little is a risky proposition, and we can hardly expect universal welcome, nor should we.

It's the same problem as Vancouver's panhandlers. Poor, desperate people are living in the midst of opulence and witnessing international travelers throwing piles of money out of the back of the bus: of course they get angry and demand some. Blatant inequality makes some people mad, and no amount of securitizing will change that. The point is that safety is always political and contingent.

△

Youth all over the world are scared of cops. Many people, and certainly the youth I work with every day, perceive police as representing the opposite of safety; they are instigators of aggression and intimidation. They are intimidated for the same reasons that kids everywhere cite: the police are intransigent and often violent. Many have a calcified value system and view inner-city youth with fear and loathing. For most poor communities, especially poor kids, and most especially poor kids of colour, cops are just another gang, well-funded and well-equipped, and with a huge army of apologists behind them.

I understand and often sympathize with this perspective. On the other hand, for many people the police are the only line of defense against domestic violence, drug-dealing thugs, predatory landlords and property theft. People with few other resources — those who are isolated, without families or neighbours they trust, people in weak physical condition, the elderly, women who are being intimidated or assaulted by their partners — rely on the police. In some circumstances, there is no question that the police can prevent the violent abuse of the weak by the strong.

But that hardly absolves them from critique. One of the core strategies police supporters use is the suggestion that those who do not advocate a vigorous police presence are therefore in favour of crime. It is the same moral simplification which suggests that if you are opposed to the Iraq war, you must be in favour of terrorism. You are with us or you are against us. We need a much more complex and vigourous discussion, and a thorough consideration of alternatives.

△

19. See as a couple of starting points for investigation the Western Prison Project (www.western-prisonproject. org), or the Centre for Restorative Justice (www.sfu. ca/crj/).

What would things look like without local policing? It is certainly true that without any kind of public safety instruments the provision of security would become as market-based as unregulated capitalism, and those with the most resources would thrive, to the detriment of those with the least. But this is not to suggest that communities without a state security apparatus will descend into a chaotic jungle of everyone-for-themselves. It is certainly possible to imagine locally delivered community security (see for just one example the development of the aboriginal restorative justice movement, or transformative justice approaches[19]), but it has to start with the assumptions that *safety is not predictable*, it must mean more than just *keeping things in their place*, and it is *always politicized*.

Assessing our fundamental assumptions about safety will lead to reconstructed notions and expectations of policing. Therefore, I am interested in the character and effect of policing *in toto*: how it governs common space, how order is maintained without police and how policing reduces public space to militarized language and relationships.

20. David Cayley, "In Search of Security," transcript of ten-part radio series broadcast on CBC Radio *Ideas* during February and March 2004, pp. 12, 15, 22.

PRIVATE POLICING, PUBLIC PLACES

Contemporary policing is only partially about the police. Today far more policing is carried out by private companies than by government-paid forces:

> In the United States today, more than 10,000 private security companies employ an estimated 2 million guards, four times the number of state and local police officers. . . . In 1985, in Brazil, public police officers outnumbered private security agents by a ratio of 3:1. Today [2004] the numbers are reversed, and the privates have the 3:1 advantage. Another country which went through a similar transition in the 1990s was South Africa, and there too private providers now predominate by the same 3:1 ratio. South Africa shares something else with Brazil as well: the same skewed distribution of wealth . . . in the early 1980s, there were already more private security officers than public police in Canada. By 1996, according to the Law Commission's estimates, two-thirds of all security providers were employed privately.[20]

It is not just a growing disparity of wealth that has driven the rise of the private policing industry; it is a transformation of how we understand distinctions between private and public space, and who is responsible for ensuring safety and security in each domain. For the CBC radio series "In Search of Security," from which the quote above comes, David Cayley interviewed criminologist Clifford Shearing extensively about this phenomenon. Shearing pointed out a vast array of places — malls, sports stadiums, office complexes, university campuses, housing estates, airports and much else — that appear to be public, but are actually privately owned and governed. They are what Shearing calls "mass private property," and understanding their prevalence is essential to understanding contemporary policing.

The numbers people give you about private security don't mean a thing because private security is not like the state police, and it's not primarily made up of specialized people with a security occupation. If you were to count private security at Disney World, you would get a very low number because you wouldn't count the Mickey Mouse, the Donald Duck, the gardener carefully making sure that there are patches you are not going to walk on because they're beautiful roses. You wouldn't count all of these people because security has become embedded in a host of functions. . . .

[Asking] "Is private security bigger or smaller than the public police?" is like counting apples and oranges. The one is a set of specialized functions. The other is a set of dispersed functions.[21]

When you talk about public security, you speak about the police, but cops operate in a larger, putatively public context. Most places where people spend their days are governed by privately hired guards and security personnel. They are everywhere: at the mall and at the desk when you enter an office building; walking around public transit platforms, parking garages, banks, art galleries, libraries, schools, universities; riding bikes around certain neighbourhoods. These folks have uniforms on. Often they carry weapons. Sometimes they're in cars. They always have fancy walkie-talkie gear. They move with a certain authority. They are not police per se, yet they are perceived essentially as cops, or at least rent-a-cops, and certainly as having a symbiotic relationship with police.

Beyond the security personnel who saturate our daily lives are what Shearing refers to as the range of people with "embedded" security functions. They imbue specific spaces with a security ethos, and the functioning of security becomes automatic in a Foucauldian sense.[22] It is, in part, our inadequate distinctions between public and private that make this possible and also shed some light on our current preoccupation with policing.

[Shearing] So, if you ask the question "Is this private space, or is this public space?" it's not as simple as it was, because the issue of access and the issue of ownership have moved out of whack. They're no longer correlated. And so, we began to talk about "quasi-public spaces" and "quasi-private spaces" and "hybrid spaces," and I began to think, with others, that these terms don't solve the problem, they just point to it.

[Narrator] . . . if it is recognized that public can be private and private public, different questions arise. The formal questions, "Who does it? Who owns it?" become less important than the substantive questions, "What actually happens? Who benefits?" . . . The critical problem, Clifford Shearing says, is not private security as such, but unequal access to secu-

21. Ibid., p. 23.
22. See in particular Michel Foucault, *The Order of Things: An Archaeology of the Human Sciences* (New York: Vintage, 1971); Paul Rabinow, ed., *The Foucault Reader* (New York: Pantheon, 1984).

rity. The solution in his view is to find ways in which poorer communities can use their own wits to secure their own peace and good order.[23]

23. Cayley, "In Search of Security," pp. 24, 26.

Is it possible that local communities might reimagine, "using their own wits," the methods private interests are effectively using to create specific security environments and apply variations to strengthen and reconstruct common space?

ARE YOU SUPPOSED TO BE HERE?

The experience of gentrification is often the way issues around safety and security are brought to a head in a neighbourhood. The flow of gentrification delineates what activities can happen in certain zones, what kind of behaviour is permissible, and who is invited to participate. Partly this environment is the result of the numbers of police and private security personnel entering the neighbourhood, but gentrification tends to be simultaneously much more subtle and more long-term in its effects.

Gentrification is what happens when a poorer, run-down or

less-developed neighbourhood is (re)discovered and colonized by capital. It forces many of the original residents to move along and changes the make-up of the community. The process is a fairly standard one: a few pioneering homeowners move into the neighbourhood and renovate character houses; a few chain stores or coffee shops establish outposts; newspapers talk about a revitalized neighbourhood; housing prices surge and rents rise; more upscale shops open up; social services relocate; police presence is increased; private security guards are hired; streets and parks become cleaner and visibly poor people are shuffled along.

Sometimes the neighbourhood is located in a physically attractive place, sometimes it is simply close to downtown, sometimes the area has been funkified by artists and radicals. Often the neighbourhood is simply too useful for those with profit on their minds to leave alone. There are classic examples in every city, from the Plateau in Montreal to the East Village in Manhattan to Kitsilano in Vancouver to the Haight in San Francisco.

An influx of capital in an older neighbourhood is not necessarily bad, and in many cases social investment or healthy business development can clearly rejuvenate an area. But in every instance, urban change comes with new discourses and expectations around safety and security. The key is to ask who is feeling secure and what kinds of activity are being made safe. As always the nature of that safety is political, and tied closely to renditions of appropriate or legitimate behaviour.

It is obvious to anyone when they enter a specific neighbourhood what kinds of behaviours are welcome, which are supported and which are not tolerated. Whether it is playing ball on the street, drinking on a park bench, driving an expensive car, not shopping, allowing the dog off the leash or letting kids yell loudly in the playground, you know how you are supposed to act, how to talk, what business you should be having and what you probably can't get away with.

Every community is laden with potent signs and securitizers. Race is the big one in most cities, but even a quick look around gives most people a clear picture of where they are. People walking around with designer shopping bags suggests a specific kind of neighbourhood, as do the kinds of dwellings, the number of people hanging around with nowhere to go, the kinds of foods people are eating, and so much else.

These signs all act as security devices, and dissonance brings attention, warning residents of unusual behaviour or people, alerting locals to possible danger, and bringing scrutiny. A broke-ass punk with dirty clothes and dreds, loud fratboys, a native kid, a new Lexus, a Hispanic family, skateboarders, a Starbucks, a woman in expensive clothes talking on a cell phone, a mother dragging three noisy kids — these all attract attention in certain places and reinforce ideas what the area considers safe, or threatening and not welcome.

24. Neil Smith, *The New Urban Frontier: Gentrification and the Revanchist City* (New York: Routledge, 1996), pp. 15, 27.

Gentrification brings competing conceptions of what constitutes a good and safe neighbourhood into conflict and plays them out in very specific arenas: rent, policing, residents' associations, garbage, drinking, etc. Neil Smith argues that gentrification is really part of a larger shift in political economy and speaks of the "revanchist" city. Smith points to the use of frontier mythology to describe the "taming" of the uncivilized urban frontiers and describes the similarities between the vocabularies of developers and those of the Wild West pioneers.

> The new urban frontier motif encodes not only the physical transformation of the built environment and the reinscription of urban space in terms of class and race, but also a larger semiotics. Frontier is a style as much as a place. . . .
> The new urban pioneers seek to scrub the city clean of its working-class geography and history. By remaking the geography of the city they simultaneously rewrite its social history as a pre-emptive justification for a new urban future. Slum tenements become historic brownstones, and exterior facades are sandblasted to reveal a future past.[24]

But it is possible to rethink gentrification using another set of ethical standards that reimagine ideals of security and risk. Consider the pride many take in defining their neighbourhood in terms of community character, style, identity, behaviour, activities. This emphasis on difference is the first step to defining identity.

The key distinction between community building and gentrification centres on the interests of capital. Community cannot be based on the buying and selling of consumer goods or on profiteering. These can be aspects of community, but not the core. Community always has to be developed around culture, around family life, around commonly held spaces. Areas that are developed as free-market zones for the buying and selling of consumer goods are not communities because the commitment is to profit and enterprise, not place or neighbours.

△

Genuine security, public or private, has to be developed through commonality. Some levels of policing may be useful in certain circumstances, but public spaces cannot be turned into contested sites regulated by police decisions. Rather, they need to be conceived as *requiring* visibility, shared ownership and responsibility as the linchpin elements of security.

Community safety has to revolve around commonality, not just publicness: shared resources and shared space. Policing might be part of the picture, but in a necessarily limited role. More police do not mean a safer community. In fact, the imposition of a militarizing discourse tends to make a neighbourhood qualitatively less secure. Reversing that trend requires recognition of the social contexts of crime and local power that enhances shared ownership and common responsibility for a place, reversing the scattering and atomizing effects of gentrification, and making sure police do not have the first, or last, words on safety. It is only through building genuine neighbourhoods that safety and security make everyday sense.

CHAPTER TEN

Every Step You Take, Every Move You Make

Official Surveillance and Monitoring

To ensure quality service and to maintain safety standards, this call may be monitored.

After each perceived security crisis ended, the United States has remorsefully realized the abrogation of civil liberties was unnecessary. But it has proven itself unable to prevent itself from repeating the error when the next crisis came along.
US SUPREME COURT JUSTICE WILLIAM BRENNAN, 1987

Those who scare peace-loving people with phantoms of lost liberty . . . your tactics only aid terrorists, for they erode our national unity and diminish our resolve . . . they give ammunition to America's enemies and pause to America's friends.
JOHN ASHCROFT, TESTIFYING AT THE US SENATE COMMITTEE
ON THE JUDICIARY'S REVIEW OF ANTI-TERRORISM POLICY,
DECEMBER 6, 2001

There is a perception that 9/11 entirely changed the way the world, specifically the West, thinks about surveillance: how much is acceptable or even necessary, what can be gathered and kept, how we can be monitored. It is certainly true that, post-9/11, governmental tracking and monitoring of citizens leapt forward, but digital technologies, state suspicions of domestic subversion, data collection capacities and deeply conservative political values had already combined to create an atmosphere in which virtually any level of data collection could be, and was, justified in terms of security.

Today there is constant observation of everyday citizens by a dizzying array of local, regional, national and international forces.

The surveillance industry is in the midst of an era of incredible growth: the Total Information Awareness office, Canadian Security and Intelligence Service, urban surveillance, border controls, closed-circuit televisions, shared data collection, bank monitoring, and the taping of telephone conversations combine to form a quilt of near-total coverage. The ubiquity and the sheer number of people observing the details of our lives has left most of us resigned to the idea that very little is genuinely private and that if someone wants to find out something about us, it probably won't be too difficult.

Great Britain, for instance, has an "estimated 2.5 million closed-circuit television cameras, more than half operated by government agencies, and the average Londoner is thought to be photographed 300 times a day."[1] These numbers have taken on added significance since the cameras failed to prevent the 2005 London subway bombings, though they did make it possible to identify the culprits quickly, suggesting that the number of cameras will be rising quickly and steadily for the foreseeable future.

[Narrator] Consider for example the Communications Security Establishment. Largely unknown to Canadians despite its nearly 900 employees and $100 million budget, it conducts so-called "signals intelligence," sweeping international communications networks for messages of interest to the government of Canada. After September 11th, the CSE gained a power it had previously lacked: the right to monitor communications originating in Canada. But the organization has existed in its present form since the 1970s when it became part of an international surveillance network comprising the United States, Great Britain, Australia and New Zealand. . . .

[Mark Perry] What they have established is listening centres in key points around the world that can intercept electromagnetic communications and very sophisticated computers. Mainly large databases, and software that can scan content for key words. . . .

[Narrator] Is all telephone intercourse in Canada under surveillance, in that sense?

[Perry] Yes. It sounds incredible but yes. Potentially, everything that goes through a telephone or a cell phone or a computer network is sniffable and inspectable by one of these agencies.[2]

The logic behind the imposition of these surveillance technologies tends to be circular, much like that of compulsory schooling. They're for your own good, and when they're not working well enough, well, you must need more. In our current political atmosphere, almost everything becomes justification for repeating

1. Michael Sniffen, "US Develops Urban Surveillance System," Associated Press wire report, July 1, 2003.
2. David Cayley, "In Search of Security," transcript of ten-part radio series broadcast on CBC Radio *Ideas* during February and March 2004 p. 94. Mark Perry teaches law and computer science at the University of Western Ontario.

WATCH YOURSELF

HOMELAND SECURITY IS EVERYONE'S RESPONSIBILITY GET INVOLVED!

157

EVERY STEP YOU TAKE, EVERY MOVE YOU MAKE

FOR IMMEDIATE POLICE RESPONSE CALL 911

REPORT TIPS TO THE TOLL-FREE PA TERRORISM TIP LINE
1-888-292-1919
OR VIA EMAIL TO
SP-INTELLIGENCE@STATE.PA.US

PENNSYLVANIA STATE POLICE
TROOPER

the cycle. As Canada's privacy commissioner, Jennifer Stoddart, commented in her 2004-05 report to Parliament,

> *Privacy threats seem to be multiplying like a bad virus, threatening to overwhelm us. . . . [There is] a voracious appetite for personal information and surveillance that has sprung up in the post-9/11 environment . . . . The machinery of anti-terrorism is being used to meet the needs of everyday law enforcement, lowering the legal standards that law-enforcement authorities in a democratic society must meet.[3]*

When Boston hosted the Democratic National Convention in July 2004, for example, the city was deemed a terror target, and a massive police and security presence was needed. The city was blanketed in surveillance cameras at a cost of $50 million for the four-day convention. Dozens of cameras were installed at every strategic point in the city, in addition to the thousands already in use by transit, transportation and police authorities. The harbour, city hall, the stadiums, the river, major streets and plazas, financial buildings . . . everything was monitored.[4]

Aside from the massive, entwined and murky relationship between local, state and national authorities, the most interesting aspect of the story is how the cameras, sold to the public as a unique requirement for the convention, stayed in place afterward. Security and surveillance was ratcheted right up, and people bought it because of the supposedly increased threat. But then it never went away.

> *And while many of the cameras are being set up in time for the convention, they will stay in use long after the delegates have gone home.*
> *"We own them now," Boston Police Superintendent Robert Dunford said. "We're certainly not going to put them in a closet."[5]*

In 2004, *Reason* magazine, a libertarian monthly with approximately 40,000 subscribers, brilliantly demonstrated the ubiquity of surveillance tools. Using only technology and search devices readily available to anybody, editorial staff at *Reason* were able to track down satellite photographs of every one of their subscribers' homes. Every copy of the magazine was customized with one of these images so that subscribers received their June 2004 issue with a picture of their own residence on the cover. The thrust of the core article was that we now live in a database nation, and privacy is a quaint relic.

In a February 2003 Harris poll, 69 percent of those surveyed agreed

3. Michael Den Tandt, "Privacy Has Suffered Since 9/11 Report Says," *Globe and Mail*, October 7, 2005, p. A6. The report was released on October 6, 2005.

4. Associated Press wire report in the *Times-Argus* (Montpelier, VT), July 19, 2004, p. C3.

5. Ibid.

6. *Reason*, June 2004.

WATCH YOURSELF

that "consumers have lost all control over how personal information is collected and used by companies." That view was summed up with cynical certitude by Sun Microsystems CEO Scott McNealy. "You have zero privacy anyway," he said a few years ago. "Get over it."[6]

It was a perfectly conceived and executed project. Libertarians of *Reason*'s ilk tend to use this kind of analysis to support the dismantling of government services in favour of free-market autonomy for corporate agendas: "Living in a database nation raises innumerable privacy concerns. But it also makes life easier and more prosperous. We may have kissed privacy goodbye — and good riddance too."[7]

SPOOKED

There is a vast and growing body of information about the surveillance of citizens and infringements of individual rights, and while much of it is germane to this chapter, I remain suspicious of conspiracy theories. There are clearly any number of ways public and private interests are maliciously using surveillance and monitoring technology right now, but the point I want to make is both more specific and more general.

Most people believe that a certain amount of surveillance is justified. That following suspected terrorists, even abroad, is the right thing to do. That closed-circuit monitoring of busy intersections is all right. That cameras in stores and banks are fine. That infiltrating suspicious political groups is justified. That the boss has a right to monitor your email. That utility companies taping your phone conversations is legal. That police cameras recording street activity in poor neighbourhoods is within reason. Everyone has a personal limit.

Behind that limit, however, lies the idea that monitoring and surveilling citizens is directly related to their own safety, that authority will act appropriately and that when the state, police or other authorities fail to ensure justice and security, it is simply because they lacked information. The argument turns in circles. In 2001 in London, as the number of surveillance cameras in public space was exploding, street crime went up 40 percent, a figure that some claimed justified the necessity of cameras: things *are* out of control. "When crime goes down, cameras get the credit; when crime goes up, it's because there aren't enough of them. Either way, the end result is more cameras."[8]

Starting from that vantage point, the debate becomes a rights vs.

7. Nick Gillespie, "Editor's Note: Kiss Privacy Goodbye — and Good Riddance, Too," *Reason*, June 2004.

8. Erin Anderson, "Smile, You're on Government Camera," *Globe and Mail*, March 30, 2002, p. F7.

GRAVELEY

SALSBURY DR 1600

BLOCK
WATCH
AREA

ALL SUSPICIOUS ACTIVITIES
REPORTED TO POLICE

4
67

safety discourse, one which has been adeptly manipulated by those in favour of virtually unfettered government power to monitor its citizens. The question becomes: Why not allow government maximum power if it will keep us safe?

△

Something happened recently that affects how I think about surveillance technologies: we got broken into. We live in a neighbourhood that has a high rate of break-and-enters, but we had never been robbed before. It wasn't that big a deal, frankly. There is always plenty of coming and going in our house, and this particular Saturday night we had some folks over for dinner and then went to bed. A teenager who was living with us (we usually have one or two) was hanging around downstairs with a friend, and shortly after we retired, the two of them went out.

Perhaps they didn't completely shut the door, or maybe somebody watched them leave, but at some point in the evening someone managed to open the front door and get into the downstairs. They took a six-pack of beer from the fridge, a visor and my favourite ball cap.[9] They rifled through Selena's jacket, finding her wallet and stealing her bank card, $50 in cash and her Visa, along with a set of keys.

The next day was a Sunday and we got up late, hung around with the kids, ate breakfast and took the day slow, meaning that we didn't discover the theft until the afternoon. Selena couldn't find her keys, and after some searching she figured out that her wallet was missing a few components. She immediately cancelled the cards and we did all the requisite things like changing the locks and talking to the teens about what happened. In short order Selena found out that at 4:00 AM someone had used the Visa to try to get cash out of the ATM on the corner. The attempt failed because she didn't have cash withdrawal services on that card.

We knew that all ATMs are video monitored, so we contacted the credit union and explained the situation. The person there directed us to the police, who urged us to file a report, which Selena did over the phone. We assumed that some combination of us, the credit union and the police would be able to view the tape and find out if the thief was someone we recognized. Our assumption was that the surveillance camera would help us deal with the break-in.

The police, however, were unwilling to investigate. It was a minor crime, and they had no interest in viewing the videotape because no money was actually stolen with the credit card. The credit union

9. The red, white and blue one from Good Hope. I'm still pissed about that.

would not let us view the tape ourselves because of privacy issues. When we went back to the police officer, whose name is prominently displayed in the credit union as the person responsible for the area and institution, she told us that ATM surveillance cameras are of no interest to them anyway because people using stolen cards cover their faces, obscure the camera or at the very least wear sunglasses and a hat pulled down low over their face. Our presumption that video surveillance would assist us was patently naïve, and we never did find out anything more.

Most of us think about surveillance and monitoring technologies or policies as a straight-up deal: we sacrifice privacy rights for security. How much do we want of one or the other, what is a reasonable balance? But what if that equation doesn't work? What if surveillance is not about safety but about something else entirely?

We may be led to feel safe, and therefore be willing, as Alexander Hamilton predicted 215 years ago, to relinquish our rights. But feeling safe is not the same as being safe, as our history repeatedly teaches us. . . . When rights are violated in the name of safety, most often we lose both our rights and our safety.[10]

If authorities are going to record everyone all the time, taking pictures and video as we go about the streets and monitoring every cell-phone call and e-mail, how many people will be needed to watch and listen? Is half the population going to watch the other half, and then switch places? Who is going to watch who?

△

Threading its way through the discourses about video and camera surveillance is the implicit assumption that captured images are a certain kind of Truth. The way different people interpret different images, what they look for and what they notice, however, are always political, and the idea that pictures will infallibly settle debates and establish facts is dated at best. I am not suggesting that authorities will doctor photos or video, but I want to emphasize the inherent subjectivity of images: they are always open to interpretation.

Take, for example, the photograph. Until relatively recently, a photograph was commonly assumed to represent the "truth" about something. If something could be photographed, that was typically deemed to be evidence of its reality. Sure, there were famous hoaxes, like the photos of fairies or the Loch Ness Monster, that

10. Ira Glaser, "More Safe, Less Free: A History of Wartime Civil Liberties," in *It's a Free Country*, Danny Goldberg, Victor Goldberg and Robert Greenwald, eds. (New York: Thunder's Mouth Press, 2003), p. 33.

WATCH YOURSELF

triggered widespread debate, but essentially a photo was seen as proof. Since the development of Photoshop, high-quality home photo printing and other digital software, however, anyone with a modicum of computer capability can put a horse's head on Britney Spears's body, a squash on top of the White House, or a gun in my hand. A photo just isn't a photo anymore.

By the same token, a video was once presumed to be infallible, but that belief has also been undermined: not only by digital technologies that can edit film and video seamlessly, but by general suspicions of the film medium, the subjectivity of the camera operator, and its inherent spectacular quality. The Rodney King trial in 1992 was one of those transitional moments where the limits of videotape were made clear. Everyone saw the footage of King being beaten by members of the LAPD. Everyone clearly saw a defenceless man punched and kicked repeatedly, long past the point when any force was required to subdue him. Everyone saw it go on and on.

A jury a short time and distance away watched that same video over and over. It was clear and certain evidence, it was truth, and yet the jury saw fit to exonerate the police involved on the basis that the video did not show events preceding the beating, which the officers claimed precipitated the situation.

In the wake of this verdict, there were riots in Los Angeles and protests across the Unitd States. Video from security cameras filming the riots was used for months afterward to identify and convict looting suspects. There was little mention of preceding events then.

USEFUL DATA

As with policing, there is vastly more going on with surveillance and monitoring than simply "watching for bad guys." It is not just cops and security professionals and the FBI watching everybody all the time. The surveillance and monitoring of everyday behaviour has extended into social services, welfare and unemployment insurance, worker's compensation, the jobsite and the service industry.

Wal-Mart, for example, maintains a staggering database on its customers. The company relentlessly documents all of the approximately 100 million customers who daily come through its 3,600 US stores, tracking everything from their social security and driver's licence numbers to their buying habits and tendencies.

By its own count, Wal-Mart has 460 terabytes of data stored on Teradata

11. Constance L. Hays, "What They Know About You," *New York Times*, November 14, 2004, pg. 3.1.

12. Ibid.

mainframes, made by NCR, at its Bentonville headquarters. To put that in perspective, the Internet has less than half as much data, according to experts.

Information about products, and often about customers, is most often obtained at checkout scanners. Wireless handheld units, operated by clerks and managers, gather more inventory data. In most cases, such detail is stored for indefinite lengths of time. Sometimes it is divided into categories or mapped across computer models, and it is increasingly being used to answer discount retailing's rabbinical questions, like how many cashiers are needed during certain hours at a particular store.

All of the data are precious to Wal-Mart. The information forms the basis of the sales meetings the company holds every Saturday, and it is shot across desktops throughout its headquarters and into the places where it does business around the world. For the most part, Wal-Mart hoards its information obsessively.[11]

Did you notice that stat? The volume of data Wal-Mart keeps on its customers is equivalent to *twice the total Internet!*? Management uses it to predict which stores will need what when, to predict consumer patterns, to ensure that supply is always on hand to answer demand, and for other critical issues. For example, in advance of hurricanes the data allows Wal-Mart to predict what customers will need: beer and Pop-Tarts.

Hurricane Frances was on its way, barreling across the Caribbean, threatening a direct hit on Florida's Atlantic coast. Residents made for higher ground, but far away, in Bentonville, Ark., executives at Wal-Mart Stores decided that the situation offered a great opportunity for one of their newest data-driven weapons, something that the company calls predictive technology.

A week ahead of the storm's landfall, Linda M. Dillman, Wal-Mart's chief information officer, pressed her staff to come up with forecasts based on what had happened when Hurricane Charley struck several weeks earlier. Backed by the trillions of bytes' worth of shopper history that is stored in Wal-Mart's computer network, she felt that the company could "start predicting what's going to happen, instead of waiting for it to happen," as she put it.

The experts mined the data and found that the stores would indeed need certain products — and not just the usual flashlights. "We didn't know in the past that strawberry Pop-Tarts increase in sales, like seven times their normal sales rate, ahead of a hurricane," Dillman said in a recent interview. "And the pre-hurricane top-selling item was beer."[12]

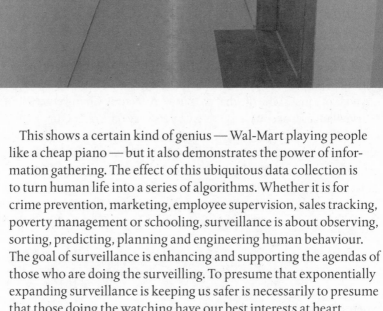

This shows a certain kind of genius — Wal-Mart playing people like a cheap piano — but it also demonstrates the power of information gathering. The effect of this ubiquitous data collection is to turn human life into a series of algorithms. Whether it is for crime prevention, marketing, employee supervision, sales tracking, poverty management or schooling, surveillance is about observing, sorting, predicting, planning and engineering human behaviour. The goal of surveillance is enhancing and supporting the agendas of those who are doing the surveilling. To presume that exponentially expanding surveillance is keeping us safer is necessarily to presume that those doing the watching have our best interests at heart.

△

As discussed in Chapter 1, Ian Hacking has documented the erosion of determinism and the development, then the explosion, beginning in the Napoleonic era, of governmental collection of printed statistical data on its citizens.

Enumerations in some form have always been with us, if only for the two chief purposes of government, namely taxation and military recruitment. Before the Napoleonic era most official counting had been kept privy to administrators. After it, a vast amount was printed and published. . . .

The systematic collection of data about people has affected not only the ways in which we conceive of a society, but how we describe our neighbour. It has profoundly transformed what we choose to do, who we try to be, what we think of ourselves. . . .

It is now common to speak of information and control as a neutral term embracing decision theory, operations research, risk analysis, and the broader but less well specified domains of statistical inference. We shall find that the roots of the idea lie in the notion that one can improve — control — a deviant subpopulation by enumeration and classification.[13]

The notion of controlling subpopulations has been expanded considerably beyond deviance mapping and maintenance. Places like Wal-Mart (in fact any store that offers a club card or scans its products — everyone is trying to emulate Wal-Mart) have realized they can track all of their customers' purchases and buying habits. We are now being counted, surveilled, monitored, enumerated and classified by a huge range of private and public bodies, each of them hoping to predict and direct our behaviours.

And that's just some of what we know. As Nancy Chang writes, "Surveillance is, of course, secretive by its very nature."[14] Our knowledge of what governments and corporations are doing and planning is necessarily always lagging behind reality. The US Patriot Act has expanded American and international surveillance capacities, and when that capacity is combined with new technologies, the monitoring of citizens is often entirely unfettered. Courts and legislation cannot keep up with cultural and political demands for security.

There is no particular value in documenting the broad and flexible powers of the Patriot Act and similar legislation across the globe, in part because it is done so thoughtfully and in such detail elsewhere,[15] in part because the landscape continues to undergo volatile surges. But as we consider the proliferation of surveillance in both the micro and macro, I want to address the assumptions behind our allowing governments, police and corporations to watch over us.

CODE ORANGE: SAFETY IN A TIME OF WAR

The omnipresent conversations throughout President George W. Bush's first term and the 2004 election campaign revolved around

13. Ian Hacking, *The Taming of Chance* (Cambridge: Cambridge University Press, 1990), pp. 2–3.

14. Nancy Chang, *Silencing Political Dissent: How Post-September 11 Anti-Terrorism Measures Threaten Our Civil Liberties* (New York: Seven Stories Press, 2002), p. 48.

15. See, for example, Cynthia Brown, ed., *Lost Liberties: Ashcroft and the Assault on Personal Freedom* (New York: New Press, 2003); Elaine Cassel, *The War on Civil Liberties: How Bush and Ashcroft Have Dismantled the Bill of Rights* (New York: Lawrence Hill, 2004); Seymour M. Hersh, *Chain of Command: The Road from 9/11 to Abu Ghraib* (New York: HarperCollins, 2004).

security, and Bush is said to have won a second term because he made Americans feel safer. The crudest explanation is that Americans felt Bush was the candidate most likely to protect US cities from direct 9/11-style attacks and to insulate American citizens from the vagaries and presumed irrationalities of fundamentalist Islamists.

In the first post-election issue of the *New Yorker*, however, Hendrick Hertzberg pointed to an interesting phenomenon. The 2004 election was remarkable in that coastal and urban Americans voted overwhelmingly for the Democratic candidate, John Kerry, while the centre and south of the country, dominated by small-town and rural voters, backed the Republican Bush. More specifically, the two cities that had come under direct attack on September 11, 2001 — New York and Washington, DC — voted overwhelmingly for Kerry.

> *Here in the big coastal cities, we have reason to fear for the immediate safety of our lives and families — more reason, it must be said, than residents of the "heartland," to which the per-capita bulk of "homeland security" resources, along with extra electoral votes, are distributed. It was deep-blue New York (which went three to one for Kerry) and deep-blue Washington, D.C. (nine to one Kerry), that were, and presumably remain, Al Qaeda's targets of choice.*[16]

16. Hendrick Hertzberg, "Blues," *New Yorker*, November 15, 2004, p. 33.

17. Tariq Ali, *The Clash of Fundamentalisms: Crusades, Jihad and Modernity* (London: Verso, 2002).

18. "The fact that Canada hasn't suffered a terrorist attack after 9/11 is largely luck, not good planning and preparedness, says a Senate report. 'When it comes to national security and defense — issues that are not part of the everyday lives of most

What Hertzberg pointed out is that the fear of terrorism and concern with security, which should be most intense in New York and DC, was expressed very differently there. Conservative Bush voters in the American "heartland" perceived that an aggressive war on terror, an invasion of Iraq and heightened military poise were the best ways to ensure security. Middle America was voting to keep its urban, coastal compatriots safe — except that those same people disagreed profoundly about what would make them feel safer.

Clearly the War on Terror was the central component of the 2004 election, but so was the "culture war" that sits at the core of the most important American cleavages — schisms that are mirrored worldwide. This war might be described in many ways: traditional vs. (post)modern, urban vs. rural, liberal vs. conservative, secular vs. evangelical. Tariq Ali called it a "clash of fundamentalisms" that is consuming much of the world.[17] Time and again it is safety to which these arguments return, often from disparate sides: environmental safety, national security, fear of crime, fear of the Other, safeguarding our values, protecting our way of life. It is not just terrorists that Bush is protecting America from.

HOMELAND SECURITY

POLICY INSTITUTE GROUP, INC.

Certificate of Membership

This is to witness that: Through the authority vested in me by
The Homeland Security Policy Institute Group
Board of Directors; it is made known and attested that

John Q. Patriot

Has so well merited as to be proclaimed publicly as having
Completed the Requirements for membership in:
The Homeland Security Policy Institute Group, Inc.

In testimony whereof I subscribe my name and affix the seal of
Homeland Security Policy Institute Group, Inc. on this day:

August 12, 2004

WATCH YOURSELF

168

_____

Managing Director, Homeland Security Policy Institute Group, Inc.

The language of war, which was central to the election, makes transparent the politicization of safety and the degree to which a United States rife with hysteria is disfiguring much of the globe. In the age of a single superpower, how Americans interpret "safety" has enormous consequences around the world. An examination of the safety rationales for the War on Terror — and its predecessor, the War on Drugs — demonstrates how our essential thinking about safeness can be instrumentalized.

There is a clear connection between how we construct definitions of safety and how we then justify specific behaviours based on those definitions. Once we make assumptions about the primacy of our security, almost anything is justified, from arcane rules for kids, gated communities and crazy lawsuits, to constant surveillance and unjustified wars of occupation. The safety-first thread runs through it all.

The core thrust of economic globalization is to make Americans safe everywhere by creating a one-world, 24/7 marketplace that is familiar, comprehensible and navigable. It is the Wal-Martization of the globe, which begins to explain why the billions upon billions of dollars being spent on the "reconstruction" of Iraq are not about rebuilding an Iraqi society based on its own best traditions and cultures. Reconstructing Iraq is really about making Baghdad look like Phoenix or Orlando, and it is just the most recent example of contemporary militarism serving a globalized economic agenda. Bush's democracy means Wal-Marts and Mickey D's everywhere — everywhere a potential investment opportunity, with the requisite security.

How we think about security and safety underlie and rationalize what we think about war. Western preoccupations with personal safety and the urge to make the world predictable are constantly referenced by, and rationalize, the War on Terror. But we live in an endlessly diverse and complex world and so are constantly confronted by risk.

WINNING THE WAR, SCREWING THE PEACE

The panicked calls to search every incoming container arriving in every US harbour, to track the movements of every citizen, to screen every piece of mail, to "civilize" every corner of the globe are, by definition, futile in terms of achieving their stated goals,[18] but in another sense they represent the successful extension of a certain ideology of surveillance and control. They make sense of US Secre-

Canadians — the vast majority of citizens trust in luck,' the national security and defense committee said Wednesday. 'Unfortunately, luck is notoriously untrustworthy.'" Stephen Thorne, *Canadian Press Report*, December 8, 2004.

19. John King, "Paige Calls NEA 'terrorist' organization," CNN, February 24, 2004 (edition.cnn.com/2004/EDUCATION/02/23/paige.terrorist.nea/).

20. On "Late Edition with Wolf Blitzer," CNN, March 9, 2003.

tary of Education Rod Paige's description of his country's largest teachers union as a "terrorist organization"[19] and Pentagon Defense Policy Board chair Richard Perle's accusation that investigative reporter Seymour Hersh is "the closest thing American journalism has to a terrorist."[20] Terror is now defined as that which gets in the way of free-market military or commercial expansionism.

The War on Terror recasts opposition to the invasion of Iraq or the Patriot Act as wilfully putting families in danger. Because they have been allowed to collapse virtually all foreign policy and internal policing into a terror rubric, the FBI, the Department of Homeland Security, Canada's CSIS, and security departments all across the globe are able to skip past discussion and debate, a phenomenon hardly confined to the United States. Secret trials, kidnapping, deportations without process, torture and suspensions of civil liberties are standard behaviour throughout the globe. The continuing willingness to accept these drastic and intensifying conditions is often described as part of "a culture of fear" precipitated by 9/11. I think it is essentially the reverse: the extension of a logic that becomes simultaneously impetus and rationale, a self-sustaining promise of safeness that can never be delivered.

21. Kucinich is an Ohio Congressman, former mayor of Cleveland and one-time sort of freaky, but excellent and charming, candidate for the Democratic presidential nomination. Quoted in Chang, *Silencing Political Dissent*, pp. 97–98.

△

The array of possibilities and the lack of safeguards and limits on law-enforcement agencies is startling, but perhaps even more disturbing is the extent to which the *Surveillance = Safety* equation has been turned inward. The Department of Justice in the United States has distributed a preparedness guide urging citizens to watch each other carefully and to report any and all "patterns of suspicious activity" to authorities and the FBI. US Neighbourhood Watch programs have been buried in money to expand their capacity to include terrorist detection. And the TIPS program (Terrorist Information and Prevention System), one of five component programs of the Citizen Corps, has enrolled up to two million American truckers, postal carriers, utility workers, public employees and rail workers in an information-gathering network, watching each other, watching everyone. As Dennis Kucinich said,

> It appears we are being transformed from an information society to an informant society. Do the math. One tip a day per person and within a year the whole country will be turned in, and we can put up a big fence around the country and we'll be safe.[21]

WATCH YOURSELF

The logic that Kucinich satirizes has taken root in safety-first soil. By 2004 Japanese parents were able to purchase GPS systems for their children's lunch bags to keep track of them, North American parents routinely track their offspring via their cell phones, employers all over the globe monitor their workers' Internet use, and various layers of security services seek to gather enough information about citizens to accurately predict behaviour. Whether it is the Total Information Awareness Office, experimental projects at DARPA,[22] video surveillance or GPS systems, the point is essentially the same: watching everyone constantly does not mean we're any safer.

The same logic gets turned and turned again until the rationales that once had meaning are obscured. If "our way of life" defines and is defined by our understanding of safety, where do the endlessly justified measures to keep us "safe" stop? How does a war without end change how we think of our culture? How can we possibly ever be completely safe, and how far will we pursue safety, knowing in advance we will fail? Safety is defined as preserving "how we live," and how we live is being determined by the needs and exigencies of safeness.

A war without end will not preserve Western culture; it will *become* the culture. Our way of life will be about defending our way of life, and a culture of permanent security will defend a society governed by predictability and probability. But I do not believe that we are at the end of history, nor do I believe that our obsession with safety cannot recede. As Isabelle Stengers says:

> Even if this history turns into a catastrophe, as is probable, it is not a question of its essence, of a fate, and thus is not a matter of faith in something beyond our history. This is why hope and thinking are technically related, because it is not fighting against reality but against probability, which is something completely different.[23]

22. US Defense Advanced Research Projects Agency.

23. Isabelle Stengers, "A Cosmo-Politics: Risk, Hope, Change," in *Hope: New Philosophies for Change*, Mary Zournazi, ed. (New York: Routledge, 2002), p. 269.

OUTRO

A World of Possibility

Those who propose avoiding risks and gaining safety will invariably find that what they acquire instead are obsessions.

FRANK FUREDI, *Culture of Fear*

Perhaps physical fears would not threaten to overwhelm citizens who felt confident of justice and social support. Perhaps people are not so much afraid of dying as death without honor. In addressing questions of appropriate risk without considering their social aspects, we could be speaking to the wrong problems.

MARY DOUGLAS, *Risk and Culture*

I hope that I am leaving you with more questions than when you started. I hope that in the end this is a book largely about hope. Far too often I see a culture that is being reduced to a grim algorithmic exercise in which risks and benefits are weighed on a positivist scale of evaluation. I see fundamental social questions being squeezed to the margins by an official culture fixated on predictability and order. I see the automatic functioning of a comprehensive safety ethos.

It doesn't have to be like this: there is a world of other possibilities. If we can continually reassert the value of public life and, more importantly, *common* life, we can rediscover the proper spheres for speaking of safety. Whether it is in taking care of our kids, facing crime or dealing with accidents, it is in the context of actual community that we can put safety in its place.

I would say that the adventure of thinking is an adventure of hope. What I mean by "adventure" is adventure as creative enterprise, in spite of the many reasons we have to despair. . . . Thus I would say that hope is the difference between possibility and probability. If we follow probability there is no hope, just a calculated anticipation authorized by the world as it is. But to "think" is to create possibility against probability . . . to think is to think against power.[1]

1. Isabelle Stengers, "A Cosmo-Politics: Risk, Hope, Change," in *Hope: New Philosophies for Change*, Mary Zournazi, ed. (New York: Routledge, 2002), pp. 245, 254.

WATCH YOURSELF

172

Here's a story about a kid named Randy Oldfield who was seventeen years old and playing for his high school hockey team in Saint John, New Brunswick. He and a teammate were chasing down an opposing player on a breakaway. Oldfield dove just as his teammate lunged, and the collision crushed his vertebrae, leaving him paralyzed and in a wheelchair for the rest of his life. It is exactly this kind of incident that has led for increasingly fervent calls to protect players, modify equipment, ban body-checking for youth, and much else.

Seven years after Randy Oldfield's accident, Toronto's *Globe and Mail* newspaper profiled twenty-four–year-old Oldfield as part of a series on safety in hockey. The reporter conducted much of the interview while Oldfield was watching and cheering a Senior A men's game. He spoke about the accident, the catastrophic changes to his life and how he has adjusted. You might think he would be a crusader against hitting in hockey. But he's not.

> *Accidents, like mine, are flukes and can always happen, but they have nothing to do with hitting. You're always going to have injuries in hockey. The goal should be to minimize them. . . .*
>
> *Hitting is part of the game. I like the hitting and fighting. It wouldn't be hockey otherwise. You don't want to see anyone getting hurt. But if you take that kind of effort away then hockey is nothing more than glorified ice skating.*[2]

Sometimes, maybe most of the time, safer just isn't better. There are other ways to think about our lives than reducing them to calculated existences with the occasional gamble. It is necessary to think of life as possibility, not probability. It is a requirement of imagining and reimagining the world.

2. Shawna Richer, "Hockey Fan Still Praises the Value of a Good Hit," *Globe and Mail*, December 4, 2003, p. S1.

INDEX

education; schools
cyberspace. *See* Internet

de Kerckhove, Derrick 126
defensible space theory 26–28
defibrillator 30, 35
democracy: community 58–59,
60–61, 63, 143, 153; driven by safety
considerations 17–19, 23, 100;
Internet 126–27; law enforcement
158; technology 35–36, 115, 116n9,
124, 128; in schools 86–87, 91–93,
95. *See also* authority; community;
public space
Democratic National Convention
(2004) 158
Dennison, George 51
Descartes, René 81
Didion, Joan 132
Dillman, Linda M. 164
Dillon, Sam 92n14
discontinuity 131–33
Disneyland 132–33
Disney World 149
domesticity 34
Douglas, Mary 5, 6
Dunford, Robert 158
Dyson, Esther 65n21

Eagleton, Terry 83
Economist 137
education: act of depositing 93; legitimizing identity 92. *See also* schools
Ellul, Jacques 114
Emami, Tara 75–77
environmentalism 71, 77, 79. *See also*
nature
ethics: community 64, 152; definition
18; dictated by probability 18, 23;
transformed by/transforming technology 115, 129; trumped by safety
18, 86. *See also* values
Ewald, F. 100n1

Fantasyland Hotel 132
fear: driven by media 9, 16–17;
encouraged by political system 9;
free-floating 8–9; of nature 81–82;
parents' 10–11, 39, 45, 86–87, 171;
retreat into home 25; of technology
113, 114–16, 130; terrorism 167, 169;
of unexpected 9, 16, 119, 166–67;
wish to eliminate risk 10, 45. *See*

also abductions; accidents; crime;
police; terrorism
Feenberg, Andrew 116n9
First Nations 72–73: in Fort Good
Hope 95–96; part of natural world
81
first nature (biology) 72, 77, 81, 83
Fisk, Robert 143–44
Ford, Henry 31
Fort Good Hope 95–96
Fossil SPOT wristwatch 113n1
Fotopoulos, Takis 124
Foucault, Michel 20, 85, 149n22
Frankenstein's monster 114
Frederick, Howard 127n36
freedom: for children 10–13, 42–46,
49, 51; corporate 110; for elite 66;
provided by technology 31–33, 122,
129, 130. *See also* surveillance
Freire, Paulo 93
front porches 28
Furedi, Frank 8–9, 20

Geddes, Patrick 59
General Motors 32
gentrification 135, 150–52
Ghermezian, Nader 132
Giddens, Anthony 5
Gladwell, Malcolm 118, 119
Glaser, Ira 162n10
global risk 116
global village 66, 114
globalization: at odds with local
places 65–66; conformity 92–93,
95, 97, 114; making Americans safe
167, 169
government. *See* authority
governmentality 85
Graham, Gordon 127
Grant, George 129
Gray, John 67
Great Britain: increase in crime 159;
surveillance 156. *See also* London
Greenberg, Dan 12

Hacking, Ian 17, 85, 165–66
Hamilton, Alexander 162
Hamilton-Paterson, James 144–45
Harper, Stephen 138, 141
Headrick, Daniel 128
Heidegger, Martin 114
Heilmann, Klaus 9n14
Hern, Matt: childhood 10, 48;

See also ethics

Vancouver: panhandlers 136–38, 146; policing 141

videos. *See* safety videos

virtue. *See* values

Voykin, Paul 28–29

Wallace, David Foster 54–55

Wal-Mart 163–64

War on Terror 16, 170: making U.S. secure 166–67, 169

weeds, immoral 28–29

West Edmonton Mall 132

Western culture: abdicating responsibility 22, 23, 26–28, 61–62, 77, 153; ambivalence about nature 75, 77, 79–81, 82–83; ambivalence about safety 21–22; belief world can be safe 169; constructs nature 72–73, 74–75, 78–79, 81–83; culture of permanent security 171; fear 8–10, 167, 169; and globalization 57, 65–66, 169; iconicizes children 40–41, 86; imperialism 128, 146, 169; isolation 26, 36–37; litigious-ness 12–13, 15–16; 9/11 155, 170; parenting 40–41; risk averse 6–7, 21; and technology 33–37, 66–67, 82, 113, 115, 121–22, 128–29 (*see especially* Chapters 2 and 8); view of women 74–75. *See also* children; community; fear; globalization; human culture; nature; safety; surveillance; technology

White, Lynn 79

wilderness: as human construction 72–74; measure for judging civilization 74. *See also* nature

Williams, Raymond: nature 69, 78

Wilson, Alexander 79.

Winkler, Henry 42n2

Winner, Langdon 114–15

women: community as home 56; conflated with nature 74–75; controlled by men 74–75; technology and housework 35

Wordsworth, William 80

workplaces: safety regulations 7–8, 85–86, 86n4; surveillance 165, 171

wristwatches 113